THE INNER CIRCLE

THE INNER CIRCLE

Reflections on the last days of white rule

JAN HEUNIS

JONATHAN BALL PUBLISHERS
JOHANNESBURG & CAPE TOWN

DEDICATION

In memory of my friend, Eljho, and my father, Chris,
who died, in that order, the one shortly after the other,
while I was writing this book.

Published in 2007 by
JONATHAN BALL PUBLISHERS (PTY) LTD
PO Box 33977
Jeppestown
2043

ISBN: 978-1-86842-282-1

Editing and index by Owen Hendry for Wordsmiths, Johannesburg
Typesetting by Triple M Design & Advertising, Johannesburg
Set in 10.5/14pt Bembo STD
Printed and bound by CTP Book Printers, Cape

CONTENTS

INTRODUCTION

Towards the end of 2005 I visited friends of mine, Mike and Eljho, at Kleinbaai on the south-east coast. I started dictating this little book on my way there, and also while driving between work and my home in the mornings and in the evenings.

It progressed well until Eljho died on 15 December 2005. Shortly thereafter, during January 2006, my father also died. For a long time I stopped dictating, but was encouraged to continue by Frederik van Zyl Slabbert's book, *The Other Side of History*. In a very real sense his book inspired me to go back to work on mine.

I would not want this book to be perceived as a self-righteous condemnation of other people. So let me say it: I have many shortcomings. Probably more than many. I would like to believe, however, that I have sinned more frequently and more seriously against my conscience than against other people. My father would have said, in his inimitable way: 'With all piety, it is safer to sin against God than against men.'

I grew up in a house in a cul-de-sac at the edge of the forest in George South. The forest effectively divided the town in two parts. The first part of my conscious life was about missing my father, a busy young attorney and community person. I got many expensive gifts from him, such as had seldom been seen in a small town like George. He had a small yacht built for me, gave me a tricycle with a little bakkie, also specially built for me, a bicycle much too large for me, a scooter with air-filled wheels, and a weird-looking three-wheeled whatever. I gave virtually all these things to the children of Standers-gang, very poor people who lived a block or two away from where I lived. I remember at least one occasion when my mother went to retrieve some of these gifts. I suppose I got all these fancy presents because my father felt that he had to compensate for his absence.

To me my father was something of a demi-god whom I desperately missed. Our house was opposite what is known as a '*meent*', the common, as large as four rugby fields. I remember one day I called out to my father when he arrived home from work (accompanied by a friend, colleague or whatever). I was desperate for him to watch me kick and catch up-and-unders. After many sessions of practice on the *meent* I was near perfect at it. Predictably I did not catch the ball this time. I so much wanted him to watch my second effort, but he did not.

Equally predictably I made a similar hash during the only rugby game I played in that my father came to watch.

At the time I revelled in the adoration of my grandmother on my father's side. She was deeply involved in charity work, and my generosity made us allies. She unashamedly called me Jan number one, and made no bones about the fact that I was her favourite grandson. Small wonder that the others gave me such a hard time on our *meent*.

When I was young, I was blissfully unaware of the fact that my father, who was involved with the activities of many or-gans of civil society, was also the member of the provincial council for the constituency of George. PW Botha was the member of parliament. I was rudely confronted with this reality when my standard two teacher, a particularly nasty piece of work, told me out of the blue that I should not think that I was special because my father was the local MPC. I had no idea what he was talking about.

By reason of his membership of the Cape Provincial Council, my father had to attend sessions of that Council in Cape Town from time to time. One Sunday afternoon during the school holiday, shortly before he was due to leave for Cape Town for one such session, I hid in the car in a futile attempt to go with him. Predictably I was seen and told to get out of the car.

I went to sit and sulk in the lounge where my mother found me and told me to go and get ready because my father was coming to pick me up. I actually went with him to Cape Town for the week.

When I was 13, my father became a member of the executive committee of the Cape Provincial Council, as a result of which the family had to move to Cape Town.

Thus we went to live in an official residence in Newlands, and I started attending the Groote Schuur High School at the commencement of the second term of my standard seven year. I saw even less of my father, since he travelled to George and back every weekend (on one occasion three times during a single weekend) to be in his constituency.

I was desperately unhappy in the new school, and missed my friends in George and the forest in which I used to play for many hours of the day, frequently by myself.

Despite being extremely unhappy, however, I was, for some

reason, voted head boy of the school as well as the pupil who meant the most for other pupils, in my matric year.

To all intents and purposes I left home at the end of matric. After doing my military service, I enrolled for a law degree at the University of Stellenbosch. During weekends I would almost invariably go to George. In the beginning I hiked, and later I used my own car, a Volkswagen 1200.

At Stellenbosch I immediately became involved in student politics. Since Piet Vorster and I were classmates and shared an interest in politics, I got to know his father, Prime Minister John Vorster. On a personal level, I found him to be a very likeable person.

During my university vacations I worked as a reporter at a local newspaper in George called the *George & Knysna Herald*. During this time, the first half of the seventies, I became good friends with Martin Botha, an excellent chef and a so-called Coloured. I attended his wedding in the 'Coloured' township of Pacaltsdorp, and proposed a toast to the bridal couple. The following week, this was prominently reported in the *George & Knysna Herald*'s main competitor, the *Het Suidwestern*, under a headline to the effect that Chris Heunis's son had attended a Coloured wedding. By that time my father had become a minister in John Vorster's cabinet, and the fact that I attended the wedding was considered newsworthy!

On leaving the university, I joined the Department of Foreign Affairs as a law adviser, and subsequently became Chief State Law Adviser in the State President's Office. A few stories in this book relate some of my experiences during this time.

Whilst in private practice as a member of the Cape bar, I was appointed to advise the government during the Kempton

Park negotiating process which culminated in the adoption of South Africa's first fully democratic constitution in 1993. The majority of the other stories relate to my experiences during this period.

Not long before my father died, PW Botha phoned him to suggest that he should read a certain autobiography. My father responded by telling him that he did not read books written by people about themselves. This book is not about me. It is about some people whom I met and events that I witnessed during my sojourn at university and my subsequent career as adviser to the government. The object of the book is, first and foremost, to share with the reader a few self-contained stories about these people and events.

Secondly, it seeks to provide the answers to some unanswered questions; for example, why PW Botha's Rubicon speech did not, to put it mildly, measure up to expectations.

Thirdly, I hope that it will put certain events of historical significance in better perspective.

The stories are in chronological order, and, since it is the idea that the reader should be able to read those of his or her choice and not necessarily all of them, there is a certain amount of repetition.

So this book is not intended to be about me. However, I suppose that in one way or another every book is, to a greater or lesser extent, about its author, particularly if it relates true encounters.

CHAPTER 1

SAMPIE TERREBLANCHE –
*friend, broederbonder, socialist,
historian, economist, etcetera*

What shall one say about the enigmatic Sampie Terreblanche, once my father's best friend? He is an emeritus professor of economics at the University of Stellenbosch, the so-called cradle of Afrikaner intellectualism and the (past!) breeding ground of Afrikaner/nationalist leaders.

To this day Terreblanche presents himself as a fighter for the interests of the down-trodden and the poor – those who have become ensnared in what Prof. Christoff Hanekom, during his lifetime professor in anthropology, a special friend of both myself and my father, and a colleague of Terreblanche, in the seventies had styled the 'culture of poverty'.

I think that Terreblanche relishes the fact that he is controversial, and despite his retired state he manages to stay in the news – most recently because of his criticism of the ANC's neglect of the poor. However, Terreblanche's current views on the political/economic/social situation in the country are not the reason for the inclusion of this chapter. It has to do with my own encounters with Terreblanche, particularly during the seventies when I was a student at the University of Stellenbosch.

Terreblanche was a prominent member of the Broederbond, an elitist, secret Afrikaner organisation of which it was often said that it wielded enormous power within the state hierarchy. In my own, albeit very limited, exposure to its activities, this is a vast exaggeration, but that is of no significance for present purposes.

Terreblanche was also a '*hoofwag*', that is a member of the Broederbond put in charge of a group (cell) of members of the 'youth Broederbond', the '*Ruiterwag*'.

In the 1970s my father was the leader of the Youth Movement of the National Party in the Cape Province. The Youth Movement was a very active organisation which held conferences on a regular basis. It was also a liberal element within the National Party, and influenced decisions such as the opening of the Nico Malan theatre to Coloured people in the seventies.

Terreblanche was invariably invited to, and attended, these conferences, together with Prof. Willie Esterhuyse, Christoff Hanekom, Hennie Rossouw, Julius Jeppe and Gerhard Tötemeyer, a senior lecturer in political science at the University of Stellenbosch who later became a SWAPO supporter in Namibia.

Terreblanche and my father were particularly good friends, and, together with other academics who were involved in the Youth Movement, they presented a not informidable enlightened force within the National Party and the Youth Movement itself. Terreblanche read the *laudatio* when my father was awarded an honorary doctorate by the University of Stellenbosch – an award which he initiated.

I should mention in passing that, for a National Party politician, my father became a member of the Broederbond relatively late in his life, presumably because in his younger years he was a founding member of the Round Table in George where he practised as an attorney. He only became a member of the Broederbond when he was already a National Party member of the Cape Provincial Council and a member of the executive council of that Provincial Council – the equivalent of a 'provincial minister' in present-day terms.

My father had Terreblanche appointed to the Erika Theron Commission, named after its illustrious chairperson, Prof. Erika Theron. The Commission had to investigate the plight of the 'Cape Coloureds'. What he did not do was to have Terreblanche appointed as a member of the President's Council, a National Party-governed, cynical deadlock-breaking mechanism between the three legislative components of the tricameral parliament established in terms of the 1983 constitution. I suspect that this infuriated Terreblanche, particularly since Hanekom, the lesser intellect but by far the better man, was made a member of the Council.

At Stellenbosch, in the early 1970s, I soon became involved in student politics. At the end of my second year I succeeded Pierre de Villiers, a flamboyant political science lecturer who has since died, as the chairperson of the student branch of the National Party at Stellenbosch.

At the time the incumbent Student Representative Council (SRC) of the university was less loyal to the National Party than it ought to have been, according to the thinking of that party. Although the SRC had, in the past, invariably supported the National Party, the most recently elected SRC was beginning to question the tenets of apartheid dogma. Not long after leaving Stellenbosch, I fully realised that they were right.

8

Enlightened thinking, such as wanting to meet with the SRC of the ('Coloured') University of the Western Cape, incurred the wrath of Prime Minister John Vorster, causing him to remark that the SRC had fouled its own nest.

In 1973 the so-called '*verligtes*' (the enlightened ones) in the SRC had a majority of one over the more conservative element. This came about as a result of one of the conservative candidates, Lizel Visser, voting for a *verligte* candidate as SRC chairperson, and not for the conservative candidate as had been agreed by the conservatives under the watchful eye of Sampie Terreblanche. Lizel Visser had broken ranks.

When I was elected as the chairperson of the student branch of the National Party, I knew nothing about the *Ruiterwag*. I didn't even know of its existence. Notwithstanding the fact that I was the 'leader' of the Stellenbosch student branch of the National Party, the largest NP branch in the country, no attempts were made to recruit me into the organisation. To this day I am not sure what the reason was, but I suspect it was because I had chosen as my roommate an agnostic by the name of Alain Blondell, whose parents were refugees from the Belgian Congo and who put up the famous poster of Che Guevara in our room. I did not even know whose picture it was that graced the wall above my head.

During my third year at university, it was decided that the student branch of the National Party should make a special effort to regain control of the SRC. Without my knowledge, the *Ruiterwag* made the same decision.

We even invited John Vorster, to good effect, to address a public meeting at the university, and subsequently, to less good effect, PW Botha to do the same. Vorster's easy approach made him a good communicator with students, whereas Botha's hardline approach made him a bad communicator.

We mounted a concerted campaign and were represented by ten candidates. Our candidates were:

- **Piet Vorster**, the son of the then prime minister of the country. He died as an embittered young man, blaming PW Botha for engineering his father's downfall as a result of the Information scandal.
- His girlfriend and later his wife, **Retha Rossouw**, still now a lovely and gracious lady.
- **Jan Hofmeyr**, an engineering student. He died in a catastrophic explosion at AE&CI when he was still very young.
- **Johan Gelderblom**, a good friend, who is still actively involved in representative politics, now for the ANC!
- **Blikkies Blignault**, a friend of Piet Vorster whom I did not know particularly well.
- **Willem Doman**, who had served on the SRC the previous year, a theology student who later became a member of parliament for the Democratic Alliance.
- **Pieter Hurter**, who similarly studied theology, left the church long ago to represent South Africa in overseas countries as a cultural attaché, and is now attached to Radio Pulpit.
- **Cassie Wait,** a famous rugby player and also a theology student.
- **Hennie van der Merwe**, a junior lecturer at the time.
- **Yours truly**.

In the event the University of Stellenbosch, of which it was frequently said that where the university is today, South Africa will be in ten years, elected all of us to the SRC. (Koos Bekker, who later became a leading Afrikaans businessman, was overheard to remark at the first meeting of the newly elected SRC that it was the dumbest SRC Stellenbosch had ever produced.)

It is a matter of some interest that before an election for an SRC is held, there takes place what is known as the circus. This used to take place in the old Stellenbosch town hall, and now takes place in the DF Malan Memorial Centre. (I was a trustee of the trust that built the centre in the seventies.) At the circus, students can ask the candidates any questions they want to. In 1973 everyone was coached to the hilt, except me. I was considered to be able to take care of myself.

Preparation for the circus was crucial. The National Party's organisation was put into gear. It was very effective. People were designated to ask questions to which the candidates had prepared answers.

Max du Preez, a friend, later editor of *Vrye Weekblad* and now a political commentator, downplays his own delightful contribution in this process and on our behalf in his book *Pale Native*.

I distinctly remember that Retha Rossouw, Piet Vorster's girlfriend, had a planted question put to her about her choice of toothpaste, to which the answer provoked thunderous applause. Johan Gelderblom famously stated, to good advantage, that he was 'not ashamed to be a Nationalist'.

I was left to my own devices, and had to face a barrage of difficult questions from the residents of Wilgenhof, a student residence which, in the 'pre-election' campaign, Gelderblom and I decided not to visit. This, a few years previously, had been Van Zyl Slabbert's residence.

In the event we were given the results of the outcome of the election at Groote Schuur, the Cape Town residence of the prime minister. What was particularly reassuring to me was the fact that the inhabitants of my residence, Huis Visser, voted for me virtually without exception. That must be a record which is unlikely to be broken. I don't know that a higher percentage of voter participation had ever been recorded in a residence.

The three other candidates who were elected and constituted the 'opposition' were:

- **Leon Kuschke**, a friend whose father was the chairperson of the Industrial Development Corporation. The father was extremely intelligent, the son even more so. He now practises law in London and Cape Town.
- **Bobby Loubser**, a theology student who had served on the SRC the previous year. He died of cancer in 2005.
- **Bertie du Plessis**, also a theology student. He is not only an artist of note, but also a particularly gifted linguist.

From my perspective, the National Party had won convincingly. Within a few hours, however, this perception would be challenged as people started claiming that the victory belonged to the *Ruiterwag*.

The tradition was that shortly after the outcome of an election, the new SRC had to meet and elect an executive committee. In our case, that had to happen on the Saturday following the election. During the afternoon of the preceding Friday I was summoned to a meeting at Terreblanche's home.

My expectation was that, at the meeting, we would decide on which of us were to be elected to the executive committee. Terreblanche chaired the meeting.

He called for nominations for positions on the executive committee. He started by calling for nominations for the chairperson. I nominated Piet Vorster. He then called for a second. Johan Gelderblom, a member of the *Ruiterwag* but more loyal to me, seconded my proposal. Those were the only votes that Piet Vorster got. As the meeting progressed, Gelderblom consistently supported me and we consistently lost.

I cannot remember the sequence of events, but knew that in terms of the outcome of that 'voting' we were going to be ruled by dominees. Doman was to be the chairperson. Hurter was to be the deputy chairperson. Bobby Loubser was to be the secretary. Vorster and Hofmeyr were elected as our candidates for the other two positions, that is treasurer and additional member.

I left with a sense that everything had been predetermined, although I still did not know of the existence of the *Ruiterwag*. After the meeting I left for my parents' home. They were then living in a rented house in the Strand.

The next morning the new SRC was due to elect the executive committee. I left for Stellenbosch early, and went to Johan Gelderblom's Jonkershoek residence. When I got there, I immediately sensed that something was up.

The previous day a gentleman in my residence, Paul Kruger (also a theology student), had asked me whom I was going to vote for as SRC chairperson. When I told him Piet Vorster, he asked me if I did not know who was responsible for the fact that I had been elected. I told him that I thought it was members of the National Party, and realised only subsequently that he was suggesting the *Ruiterwag*. I remember that he tried to persuade me, to no avail, to vote for the dominees.

As it turned out Pierre de Villiers, my predecessor as chairman of the student branch of the National Party, who, rumour had it, had an axe to grind with the Broederbond because his father was never invited to be a member of that organisation, had gone to work. I am certain that, when he heard who were going to serve on the new executive committee, he realised that the Broederbond, in the person of Terreblanche, was responsible. I remember that he told me he had been to visit Kuschke early that morning and told him that the Broederbond had taken control of the process and that it was possible to broker a deal with the 'opposition' by splitting the ten of us.

Before I arrived at Stellenbosch that morning, De Villiers had managed to persuade Piet Vorster, Retha Rossouw, Jan Hofmeyr (a good friend of Vorster) and Gelderblom that the deal concluded at Terreblanche's home should be reneged upon.

His own proposal would see, *inter alia*, Vorster as chairperson, Doman as vice-chairperson, Hofmeyr as treasurer, Loubser as secretary, and me as the additional member of the executive committee.

Apart from myself, Cassie Wait was not yet part of the deal. It did not take long to convince either of us. Those who did not know of the change of plan were Doman, Hurter, Blignault and Van der Merwe. Obviously Loubser and Du Plessis knew. In the event the ten split as we voted with the members of the 'opposition' to elect the executive committee.

Terreblanche was furious when he learned of the outcome of the election. He travelled to my father's Strand home, jumped out of the car, branded me a traitor in the Lizel Visser mode, and then went in to see my father. He got more than he bargained for. He was promptly reminded that the decision regarding membership of the executive committee had been taken in my absence and that I was led to believe that the meeting in which I subsequently participated was electing the candidates for the executive committee, whereas, in truth, the *Ruiterwag* had pre-determined the outcome.

At a braai at my uncle's house the following day, my father asked me whether I knew of the existence of the *Ruiterwag*. I told him that I did not. He then told me what it was and that they were responsible for initially deciding who should be on the executive committee.

There was hell to pay at Stellenbosch. The 'ten' were summoned to the house of Kosie Gericke, the vice chancellor. Those who had broken rank were taken to task. Piet Vorster tearfully volunteered to resign as chairperson, and various others asked for forgiveness. Jan Hofmeyr and I, however, did not. We felt more cheated against than having cheated. Since we were the only (male) members of the ten who were not members of the *Ruiterwag*, this was objectively true.

By a process of resignation and re-election, effect was given to the original idea, with the exception of the fact that I did not resign as a member of the executive committee.

My father was variously the minister of Economic Affairs, Home Affairs, Transport, and Constitutional Development and Planning; and during PW Botha's illness following a stroke, the Acting State President.

In the beginning, and because they were good friends, Terreblanche would frequently make contributions to my father's speeches. I should say, for the benefit of would-be politicians, that it is not good to be dependent upon other people to write your speeches and to deliver texts that do not reflect your own thoughts. Some of the most beautiful speeches that I have ever heard (and that have made a lasting impression on my life) were made by my father when he spoke off the cuff. The Thabo Mbeki whom I came to know at Kempton Park could also do this. In my view his subsequent relative unpopularity could have been prevented had he capitalised on this ability.

During the 1980s Terreblanche severed his relationship with my father to the extent of not even making social calls.

One evening, when my son and I were returning from the South African wrestling championships in which my son had participated, I noticed Terreblanche in the business class section of the aircraft. A few days previously he had written a newspaper article in which he claimed to have written most of my father's speeches. I went to sit next to him and told him that that was untrue. In any event, and most importantly, a scholar and a gentleman never disclosed his author's role in other people's speeches. I also told him that I personally had discarded many of his inputs since I considered them not worthy of inclusion in my father's speeches. He acknowledged that he was wrong, but he has since made the same claim on numerous occasions.

In my final year I was invited, on short notice, to meet with Ds Chrisjan Brand, a parson in the student congregation of the Dutch Reformed Church. I arrived at the rectory fortified by the bottle of wine I had had with my lunch. Brand invited me to join the *Ruiterwag*. I firmly declined.

Then Piet Vorster stepped out from behind a curtain. It had clearly been anticipated that I would decline, and Piet was cleverly chosen to bring pressure to bear on me. My father was, after all, a minister in his father's cabinet.

So it was that I joined the *Ruiterwag* a few months before leaving Stellenbosch University after five years.

At my father's funeral I scanned those present in the hope that Terreblanche, for his own sake, would be there. Sadly, he was not.

CHAPTER 2

DOING TIME IN THE DEPARTMENT OF FOREIGN AFFAIRS

In 1976 the Department of Justice was home to the State Law Advisers who advised all government departments on South African law. The Department of Foreign Affairs was home to the State Law Advisers who advised all government departments on public international law.

In that year, having completed my studies at the University of Stellenbosch in 1975, I joined the legal section of the Department of Foreign Affairs as a rookie State Law Adviser.

The Minister of Foreign Affairs was an old-school diplomat, Dr Hilgard Muller.

Roelof Frederik Botha, known to all as Pik Botha, studied law at the University of Pretoria and was subsequently admitted as an advocate to the Supreme Court of South Africa. However, he would be the last to lay claim to being an outstanding or even moderately good lawyer. His most noticeable achievement at university was that he was its cheerleader, a role in which I am sure he excelled, given his exuberant and boisterous personality.

After having joined the South African Department of Foreign Affairs, he was involved in cases before the International Court of Justice in The Hague, concerning the administration of South Africa's mandate over what was then known as South

West Africa, now Namibia.

Given the fact that the South African legal teams included intellectual giants such as Ernie Grosskopf SC, Lang Dawid de Villiers QC and John Viall, Chief State Law Adviser to the Department of Foreign Affairs, it is highly unlikely that Pik Botha played a significant role in the formulation and presentation of South Africa's case. From what I have heard, he was more of a gofer than a participant in the preparation of the substantive case.

Be that as it may, he did become something of a household name in the process, and in the early seventies he was elected as a National Party member of parliament. In his maiden speech he made a plea that South Africa should accede to the International Convention on Human Rights, which caused something of a stir in National Party circles.

I remember that, during my first year at the University of Stellenbosch in 1971, he accepted an invitation to address a meeting organised by the Stellenbosch Aktuele Aangeleentheidskring (SAAK), a student organisation that strove to invite prominent South Africans across the entire political spectrum to speak at meetings that it organised.

Pik Botha was to represent the National Party, and Colin Eglin, then the Progressive Party's member of parliament for Sea Point, was invited to represent that party.

In the event Pik did not pitch, citing as the reason the lame excuse that he was prevented from doing so by the chief whip of the National Party in parliament.

When I joined the legal section of the South African Department of Foreign Affairs in 1976, Pik was South Africa's ambassador to the United Nations. The legal section comprised John Viall, who was the Chief State Law Adviser, and Piet Oelofson and George Barrie, who were Viall's deputies. Viall was an exceptionally studious person with a keen intellect, and one of the best law advisers I ever had the privilege to work with. Both Oelofson and Barrie were former professors of law, Oelofson at the University of Natal and Barrie at the Rand Afrikaans University. They were also legal scholars of note, and I learned a lot from all three of them.

During 1976 Pik Botha made a very progressive policy statement in the Security Council of the United Nations which was widely reported and acclaimed in so-called enlightened (*verligte*) political circles in South Africa. Although Pik got all the credit for the speech, it was written by John Viall.

In 1977 Muller resigned from active politics and Vorster appointed Pik as his successor. This appointment was widely welcomed, and *Rapport*, an Afrikaans Sunday newspaper, suggested in its main front-page article that Pik was destined to become Vorster's successor as South Africa's prime minister. That certainly did not endear him to many of his colleagues, although he was well liked by Prime Minister John Vorster.

Following his appointment, Pik wasted no time in surrounding himself with some of the more competent officials in the Department of Foreign Affairs, such as Niel van Heerden, Derek Auret and Herbert Beukes.

To his credit, Pik was not intimidated by sharp minds. He used them to his best advantage although he did overlook the most competent official in the Department of Foreign Affairs at the time, Sean Cleary. Cleary, later a political counsel at the South African embassy in Washington, was once described to me by an American visitor to South Africa at a function held by Herman Nickel, the then American ambassador to South Africa, as the most skilful diplomat ever to work the Hill – a reference to Capitol Hill in Washington.

Even Dr Chester Crocker, former US Assistant Secretary of State for African Affairs, wrote in his book, *High Noon in Southern Africa – Making Peace in a Rough Neighborhood*, the following:

> In addition, Botha had seasoned talent at his side in the Department of Foreign Affairs: his own former boss, Brand Fourie, a man of sixty-five who had held the top career position since 1966. Fourie had seen nearly twenty years' service in Europe and New York, and he had advised General Jan Smuts on the drafting of the UN Charter. An understated and gentle person, with a keen tactical mind and a calm personal manner, Fourie was the perfect foil for his mercurial minister. With their able, younger associates such as Niel van Heerden (serving in Bonn in the early 1980s), Sean Cleary (serving in Washington), Riaan Eksteen and Derek Auret (the planning staff), Botha and Fourie could assemble a strong team.

Viall and Cleary were later assigned to the office of the administrator-general who had to oversee the administration of South West Africa during the run-up to independence in 1989. South West Africa cost South Africa dearly.

Predictably Pik's style of appointing perceived old cronies to his office, competent as they were, soon led to criticism in the department, as a result of which Pik called a meeting of all the departmental officials at the Union Buildings in Pretoria where he said that he was aware that he was being criticised for surrounding himself by a 'first team', the rest of the officials being members of the 'second team'. In his view, he added, he could also discern a 'third team'! He did, however, undertake to appoint people to his office on merit and not to continue to rely consistently on the advice of the same people – a promise he kept.

At the time a core element of the department had to move to Cape Town for the six-monthly sessions of parliament, which normally commenced towards the end of January, or the beginning of February. Only one law adviser was required in Cape Town and John Viall invariably went.

When Viall was assigned to the administrator-general's office in Windhoek, Piet Oelofson, the next most senior law adviser, took over this responsibility. Since he had children at high school and was very much a family man, he did not relish having to go to Cape Town by himself for six months of the year.

Up until then I had very little exposure to the secretary of the department, a small, bright and sprightly man, BG (Brand) Fourie, and even less to Pik Botha. My break came when a court application citing the departments of Police and Foreign Affairs, which also involved the government of Mozambique, was served on the department at the Union Buildings. Since neither Oelofson nor Barrie was there, Fourie had no choice but to invoke my assistance.

He was not particularly concerned with the merits of the matter, but did not want the department to be involved in court cases involving foreign governments, particularly since it had the potential of compelling the South African government to take an official stand on whether or not it recognised the Frelimo government of Mozambique as either the *de facto* or the *de jure* government of that country in circumstances where the South African Defence Force was actively involved in supporting Renamo, a guerilla movement engaged in civil war against the Frelimo government. My instructions were to extricate the department from the court case.

Counsel was appointed to represent both departments, and during consultations with them I insisted that they attempt to have the application against the Department of Foreign Affairs withdrawn on the basis that, since another department of state was also a party to the proceedings, any court judgement against the South African government would be given effect to by that department.

Negotiations with the applicants' counsel followed, and they agreed to withdraw the application against the Department of Foreign Affairs, much to Fourie's delight.

This turned out to be my big break. Whereas Oelofson did not relish the prospect of having to go to Cape Town for six months of the year, I dearly wanted to. My children were still young and could go to the primary school in Acacia Park, the parliamentary village near Wingfield in Cape Town. I also had strong ties with the Cape, having gone to school there and having studied at Stellenbosch. When Oelofson suggested to Fourie that I should be the law adviser to go to Cape Town during the forthcoming (1981) session of parliament, Fourie immediately agreed.

Shortly after the commencement of the parliamentary session in 1981, I had another break. During the Department's budget vote in parliament, Harry Schwarz, a Progressive Federal Party member, launched an attack on the department with a predominantly legal theme, and I was assigned to prepare a draft response for Pik's use.

I immediately went to the Library of Parliament, there to find that the specific book that I was looking for, a primary source which should never have been removed, had been taken out by Dr Denis Worrall, then a National Party senator who also practised law at the Cape bar. This meant that I had to go to Worrall's Keerom Street chambers to retrieve the book before I could begin preparing the draft response.

At one minute to 12 (midday having been the deadline set for me by Fourie) I presented him with my draft response, which Pik used in its entirety without changing a single sentence.

That was my second break. From then on I was very much part of the inner circle of officials upon whom Pik relied for advice. I had become a member of the 'first team', and had stepped into Viall's shoes as a Pik Botha confidant.

Pik is a flamboyant person, a shrewd politician and an excellent orator, both at public gatherings and in front of the television cameras. He is not, however, a fundamental and original thinker. This he compensated for by relying on the advice of his officials, and was a good judge of the quality of the advice.

What made it easy for a law adviser to work for him was that he never second-guessed legal advice based on his own knowledge of the law. What made it difficult was his tremendous energy and drive. He lived hard and fast, frequently drinking too much even on the eve of major international events, such as meetings of the Security Council at which he was scheduled to speak.

He liked to be in the limelight, he liked to be liked, he liked good publicity, he thrived on public adoration, and he was extremely ambitious. Predictably, he was not good at handling criticism, particularly not when it was expressed publicly. Here follow a few anecdotes to provide some insight into the character of the man.

On one occasion he participated in a parliamentary debate. Dr Frederik van Zyl Slabbert, leader of the opposition, spoke immediately after him, and commented on Pik's presentation of his speech. Slabbert said that at some point during the presentation, Pik had thrown down his prepared notes theatrically, had looked up at the press gallery, and had continued with an unprepared speech with a look of total insincerity and in the best tradition of a ham actor.

In the style of South African parliamentary debate, as in Westminster, Slabbert's comments were not particularly harsh, and in fact what he said was true. Pik, however, was furious. He summoned me to his office and instructed me to prepare a draft letter to Slabbert taking him to task for his remarks in parliament.

I prepared the draft, took it to Pik and advised him not to send it. In the event, he followed my advice.

He hated administration and paperwork, and would perform these necessary tasks which came with his responsibilities grudgingly and, quite literally, swearing loudly. Late one evening I had to wait outside his office for an appointment whilst he was reading and signing correspondence. I could hear him talking to himself and swearing loudly whilst he went about his work.

In the wake of the Information scandal, which resulted from the uncovering of secret projects of the Department of Information, including the publication with state funds of a daily newspaper, *The Citizen*, which supported government policy, the former secretary of the department, Dr Eschel Rhoodie, was charged with certain crimes.

During his trial, his ex-minister, Dr Connie Mulder, gave evidence and testified as to knowledge which Pik had of certain secret projects whilst still South Africa's ambassador to the United Nations. Again Pik was furious, notwithstanding the fact that he was not accused of anything untoward. I was entertaining friends at my home that evening when he instructed me to call the attorney general of the Transvaal provincial division of the Supreme Court, who personally conducted Rhoodie's prosecution, to convey to him Pik's willingness to testify. I told him that I would phone the attorney general, but that he was unlikely to accept the offer since Pik's evidence would not be relevant.

At his insistence, I phoned the attorney general who, predictably, told me that he was grateful for the offer but did not require Pik's testimony. I relayed this to Pik who said that he was going to make a public offer to that effect in any event, and that I should convey that to the attorney general.

When I spoke with the attorney general again, he asked me to convey to Pik that in such an event he would have to publicly reject Pik's offer and that it would cause embarrassment, particularly in circumstances where the defence had already applied for the presiding judge's recusal. I conveyed this to Pik, who instructed me to prepare a draft offer and have it ready first thing the following morning.

When I arrived at his office with the draft offer, I discovered that Pik's political adviser at the time, Herbert Beukes, was behind the idea. During the ensuing debate about whether or not Pik should make the offer, I played my trump card and told him that cross-examination would not be restricted to what he had to say in reply to what Mulder had testified, and that I did not want him to be cross-examined about what he knew, and did not know, of secret government projects while he was South Africa's ambassador to the United Nations. That did the trick. Pik immediately decided not to make the offer.

Pik had the habit of referring to officials as 'lesser lights'. I considered this to be ungrateful, ungraceful and inappropriate, particularly since many of his successes as Minister of Foreign Affairs were attributable to the unstinting efforts of the very same officials. One thinks, for example, of the conclusion of the Nkomati Accord with Mozambique, the withdrawal of Cuban troops from Angola, and the independence of Namibia.

The Nkomati Accord was a non-aggression pact concluded between the Republic of South Africa and the People's Republic of Mozambique at a time when the South African Defence Force was actively supporting the Renamo movement which was involved in civil war against the Frelimo government in Mozambique.

The first round of talks with the Mozambiquans resulted in the establishment of a number of joint working groups, among them the joint security working group on which I served. After the first meeting, I told Pik that the Mozambiquans were ready to sign a non-aggression pact, whereupon he instructed me to prepare such a draft agreement which he would then take to cabinet. That was duly done, and he obtained cabinet approval for the further negotiation of the draft agreement.

On our way to Maputo for the third round of talks, and armed with the draft agreement, Pik told me to come and

27

sit next to him in the aircraft to explain the draft agreement, which, he confessed, he had not yet read, notwithstanding the fact that he had piloted it through cabinet!

The fourth round of talks took place in Cape Town. Nothing much happened in plenary session during the course of the day, and I was instructed to draft a joint statement, which I did in double-quick time. However, the translation into Portuguese took much longer than was anticipated, as a result of which a helicopter trip around the Cape Peninsula had to be cancelled, to Pik's utter dismay.

That evening other 'lesser lights' and I negotiated with Mozambiquan ministers the text of what was to become the Nkomati Accord. We managed to finish this at three o'clock in the morning, whereupon Pik gave an impromptu speech threatening the Mozambiquans with the full might of the South African Defence Force should they not strictly adhere to the terms of the agreement. Ironically, I happen to know that after the agreement had been signed the State President, PW Botha, authorised the Minister of Defence, Magnus Malan, to deliver one more consignment of weapons to Renamo. For reasons set out by Van Zyl Slabbert in *The Other Side of History*, there were probably many more consignments.

Pik loved to play with arms and ammunition when pleasantly inebriated. On one occasion he threw ammunition into a campfire, and the bullet from one of the exploding cartridges passed through the lobe of the ear of his private secretary, Vic Zazaraj.

The Coventry Four saga was Pik's biggest public relations nightmare. In 1984 one Armscor employee and three Kentron employees were apprehended in the United Kingdom and charged with having broken UK customs and excise laws by arranging for the export, from the UK to South Africa, of parts capable of application in weapons systems, such as gears for G5 canons and voltage tunable magnetrons for Kukri missiles.

They were released on bail by the Coventry magistrate's court, and a subsequent appeal to the High Court, against the refusal of the magistrate's court to vary their conditions of bail so as to permit them to return to South Africa, was successful. They were allowed to return to South Africa on the strength of a government undertaking that they would be extradited to stand trial in the event of any of them refusing to do so voluntarily.

While they were in South Africa, a number of political activists who were being sought by the South African police took refuge in the British consulate in Durban. When the British government declined to surrender them to the South African police, the South African government resolved, in an act of reprisal, that the Coventry Four would not return to the UK to stand trial there.

Because international law is not enforced by an international police force and there were no international courts with compulsory jurisdiction, international law recognised the concept of reprisal which, simply put, renders lawful an act which would otherwise have been unlawful but which is resorted to by way of retaliation for a prior unlawful act by the state which is being retaliated against.

The South African government came in for severe criticism, and Pik tried publicly, particularly on national television, to justify the government's conduct by likening it to throwing a stone through your neighbour's window because he had thrown one through yours. This, of course, did not work, because the notion of self-help is foreign to all civilised domestic legal systems.

What he ought to have done was to explain that international law, for reasons already mentioned, recognises reprisals as being lawful even though the concept is foreign to domestic legal systems.

Pik, heavily criticised even by newspapers normally supportive of the government, decided that I should go on national television and explain the concept. The interview was scheduled to take place in his office, but upon the arrival of the SABC broadcasting team, always only a phone call away, Pik decided to give it another go himself, failing yet again to emphasise the differences between international law and domestic legal systems and the reasons for those differences.

I never saw Pik lose his temper, but once had a telephone conversation with him when he seemed really angry. During 1984, relations between the UK and South Africa were at a very low ebb as a result of the Coventry Four incident. Following the South African government's decision not to allow the Coventry Four to return to the UK to stand trial there, I had to go to London to prepare, together with Sir Maurice Bathurst, heads of argument for George Carman QC for purposes of an application to have the warrants of arrest for the Coventry Four set aside on the basis that the UK government had acted unlawfully by providing refuge in the UK consulate in Durban to six political activists wanted by the South African police.

By that time Dr Denis Worrall had replaced Marais Steyn as South African ambassador to the UK. Whereas Marais Steyn

had allowed me to handle the matter on my own with the assistance of Andre Pelser, an official at the embassy, Worrall was
a different kettle of fish.

He was desperately (and understandably) keen to ingratiate
himself with the Foreign Office, and never took the fight to
them regarding the Coventry Four issue. Instead, he attempted
to persuade the South African government to return the Coventry Four. He even attempted to solicit my support for his
view, and, in so doing, he diverted my time and energy from
my job.

Finally I got fed up and phoned Pik Botha to tell him that
the ambassador was wasting my time with what was, given the
South African cabinet's firm position on the matter, an exercise in futility.

Pik was furious, and told me to tell Worrall that he should do
his job or be recalled to South Africa. He seemed dead serious.
I simply told Worrall that I had spoken to the minister who had
assured me that there was absolutely no possibility of the South
African government changing its position on the issue.

Pik was a hard drinker and, by his own account, a woman-
iser. He would normally drink 'after hours', for example when
he would meet with his officials to strategise. As I have said,
even on the eve of very important events he would drink a lot.
However, the next morning he would seemingly be none the
worse for wear.

Except for one occasion, I never saw him drinking while
actually working. On that occasion, I had to go and discuss
an urgent matter with him at the Foreign Affairs guesthouse
in Waterkloof where he was attempting to broker a ceasefire
agreement between Renamo and Frelimo – certainly enough

to drive one to drink! He left the meeting to speak to me in the lounge armed with his tumbler of whisky. He was so drunk that the glass simply slipped from his hand and fell on the floor. I made a dash to get a cloth to wipe up the mess in a hasty but effective attempt to prevent any of the foreign visitors from seeing what had happened.

In his book *High Noon in Southern Africa*, former United States Assistant Secretary of State for African Affairs, Dr Chester Crocker, recounts how he had met a South African delegation comprising the ministers of Foreign Affairs and Defence and their advisers in Cape Verde in the context of the negotiations concerning South Africa's withdrawal from Angola. These are his words:

> The Cape Verde encounter served as a warning of things to come. One wondered about the 'policy process' among grown men who took such evident delight in making spectacles of themselves in the presence of foreigners, strangers, and their own young countrymen (and women) from South African Airways. We watched in amazement as a member of the South African cabinet wilfully delayed a SAA Jumbo Jet and then tried to intimidate its outraged commander into silence. It reminded me of another time when Gabon's president, Omar Bongo, held a UTA Jumbo on the ground in Libreville for two hours during a refueling stop in order to conduct a conversation with me. These African leaders, white and black, represented a laboratory of Lord Acton's dictum about absolute power. Some members of the Pretoria gang, when free of the scrutiny that normally accompanied high office, behaved as if South Africa and everything in it were their personal possessions. At a deeper

level, this mixture of self-indulgence and bullying was adoles-
cent. Could these guys get their act together when times got
tough and fundamental choices were needed?

Pik was not particularly good in one-on-one negotiations. As
a result of the nature of his cabinet portfolio at the time, i.e.
Foreign Affairs, his participation in the multi-party negotiations which preceded the adoption of the 1993 interim constitution was very limited. However, on one occasion he had
to go to Kempton Park to discuss with Cyril Ramaphosa the
future of the republics of Transkei, Bophuthatswana, Venda and
Ciskei, so-called independent states which were previously
part of South Africa but were granted 'independence' in pursuit of the policy of separate development.

As with many other matters, the government had a 'non-
negotiable' position as regards the future of these territories.
None of them would be obliged to opt for re-incorporation
into the new democratic South Africa. They would have a
choice, and if they elected to become part of South Africa
again, that preference would be implemented after South Africa's first democratic elections.

The ANC's position was diametrically opposed to this. Its
position was that the commencement of the new political dispensation would also involve the re-incorporation, prior to
the general election, of the TBVC states.

One afternoon the future of these 'states' was on the agenda at Kempton Park. Pik led the government's negotiating
team, and Cyril Ramaphosa the ANC's negotiating team. It
soon became apparent to me that Pik and Ramaphosa were at
cross-purposes. Pik had assumed that the ANC was aware of

the government's position. Consequently, in discussing the future of these territories they were proceeding from very different points of departure.

During a break I told Pik that they were at cross-purposes. He got on the phone to FW de Klerk there and then, and ten minutes later the ANC was told that the TBVC states would be re-incorporated prior to the commencement of the new political dispensation in South Africa.

Not long after the Coventry Four incident, a Dutch national, Klaas de Jonge, who was wanted by the South African police, sought refuge in the Dutch consulate. The Dutch foreign minister travelled to South Africa to negotiate with Pik. During a dinner which preceded the talks, Pik, obviously relishing the moment, spoke his own version of Dutch with his guests. After dinner, and shortly before the meeting with the Dutch delegation started, one of their number told me that they could not understand a word of what Pik was saying and would I please ask him to speak English!

During the Coventry Four saga a delegation of the Johannesburg bar, which included Arthur Chaskalson SC, later South Africa's chief justice, came to see Pik Botha at the Foreign Affairs guesthouse in Pretoria. The purpose of their visit was to express their dismay at the decision not to allow the Coventry Four to stand trial in the United Kingdom. Pik listened to them for five minutes and then left the meeting, leaving Piet Oelofson and me to carry the can.

Pik was the people's politician, but his colleagues would not trust him with the leadership of the National Party, a position which would have resulted in him becoming prime minister and later state president. He was a candidate on two occasions for this position, but on both occasions garnered the fewest votes. These decisions were unpopular with the public at large, and throughout his career Pik remained a crowd-puller and a much-sought-after speaker. He was an ambitious and opportunistic politician. Although he was widely regarded as a *verligte* member of the National Party barely able to associate himself with National Party policies, he never reached the point where he elected to resign his position, not even when PW Botha repudiated him for having said that he would have no problem serving under a black state president.

I remember telling him, in the parking garage of what was then the HF Verwoerd Building, about my decision to resign as Chief State Law Adviser in the President's Office over the Hendrickse affair. He was clearly embarrassed about the matter, but not prepared to cross swords with PW Botha. He only came out in open revolt against Botha, like a hyena stalking a wounded lion, when it was patently evident that Botha's days as state president were numbered as a result of his illness, following a stroke.

He was John Vorster's protege, but quickly shifted his allegiance to Botha when it became apparent that Vorster was going to have to be forced to resign as president as a result of the Information scandal.

Pik similarly came out in open revolt against Botha when it became apparent that De Klerk would force him to resign. Following the adoption of the 1993 interim constitution and the establishment of a Government of National Unity, which included certain National Party members, Pik became the Minister of Mineral and Energy Affairs in Mandela's Government of National Unity.

He served happily as a National Party member of that cabinet until De Klerk decided that the National Party would no longer participate in the Government of National Unity. That effectively ended Pik Botha's political career as a minister, causing him to switch allegiance to the ANC, no doubt in the hope that he would be offered a public position in recognition of his political 'homecoming'. That was not to happen.

Crocker refers to Botha delightfully as follows in *High Noon in Southern Africa*: 'Botha's legendary dramatic talents and his capacity to hold forth extemporaneously – leaving interlocutors numb or struggling to get a word in edgewise – were not news.'

CHAPTER 3

THE NKOMATI ACCORD –
WHAT PRICE THE STATE'S WORD?

During the late 1970s and early 1980s Mozambique's Frelimo government and Renamo, a Mozambiquan resistance movement, were waging a bloody civil war, particularly in the northern part of Mozambique.

Frelimo was a communist government and therefore, by definition, an archenemy of the South African government. Although to a lesser extent than some other countries, Mozambique also harboured members of the ANC, perceived by the South African government as a terrorist organisation. The ANC was involved in an armed struggle against the South African government in what it considered a legitimate attempt to overthrow the oppressive white minority regime.

The South African Defence Force assisted Renamo to the hilt by supplying it with arms and ammunition. At the time South Africa had a very sophisticated and advanced arms manufacturing capacity, largely as a result of the fact that it had to cater for its own needs because of a United Nations-sponsored international arms embargo.

Economically Mozambique was in dire straits and was not assisted, to any significant degree, by its patron, the Soviet Union. Inevitably it had to look to its southern neighbour for economic survival. So it came about that during December

1983 a meeting took place in Swaziland between delegations of the two countries, respectively led by South Africa's foreign minister Pik Botha and Mozambique's Canadian-born General Jacinto Veloso, Minister for Economic Affairs in the presidency.

Since it was the end of the year and parliament was due to convene in Cape Town early in the new year, a core of public servants of each government department moved to Cape Town for the duration of the parliamentary session. Being Law Adviser to the Department of Foreign Affairs, I was one of them. At the time of the meeting in Swaziland, I had taken a break to holiday with my family at my parents-in-law's home in George. From there we would go to Cape Town for the duration of the forthcoming session of parliament. On our arrival in George a message awaited me. It had been decided at the Swaziland meeting to investigate the possibility of co-operation between South Africa and Mozambique. To this end four bilateral working groups, comprising officials from both countries and from various departments of the two countries, were appointed. These included a joint security working group, with the aim of finding practical ways of eliminating all forms of aggression and subversion on both sides, and a joint economic working group to hold consultations for the best possible use of transport services and manpower, and matters relating to minerals and energy, agriculture, industry and commerce.

The message was to the effect that I had been assigned to serve on the joint security working group and had to attend the first meeting thereof in Pretoria on 7 January 1984. Ray Killen, deputy director-general of Foreign Affairs at the time, and I were the two representatives of the Department of Foreign Affairs on the security working group. The South African Defence Force was well represented by very senior officers, including General Ian Gleeson. The South African Police was represented by the Commissioner of Police, General Johan Coetzee, a conceited and pompous man with a law degree who liked to use Latin phrases as frequently as he could. He might have been a good (security) policeman, but he was an inept negotiator.

At the first meeting, held at the Foreign Affairs guesthouse in Pretoria, it soon became apparent that Mozambique was sufficiently desperate to sign a non-aggression pact or treaty with South Africa. In a very real sense such a treaty would also have benefited Mozambique economically inasmuch as South African military assistance to Renamo would have had to cease, obviously bringing with it the possibility of a speedy end to armed conflict and economic recovery in that country.

It was also immediately clear to me that the South African military component was going to stall. They had a vested interest in the matter. The business of the military is to make war. Also, Armscor's interests were at stake. After all, the South African Defence Force was its biggest client.

I made no report to Pik Botha after the meeting because I assumed that Ray Killen, being the senior, would make a report.

However, shortly after my arrival in Cape Town I met Pik Botha in the passage of the 17th floor of the HF Verwoerd Building, as it was then known, where the Department of Foreign Affairs' parliamentary component was housed. I told him that I assumed that he had been briefed, but that I would gladly share with him my impressions if he wanted to hear them. Naturally he did. I told him that it was my impression that Mozambique would sign a non-aggression treaty with South Africa, but that the South African military component was going to attempt to avoid that at all costs.

Shrewd as he is, Pik Botha suggested that I should prepare a draft agreement which he could take to the cabinet, saying that one always had an advantage if one had a document.

That was an assignment I enjoyed, because I could draw on various treaties, and the United Nations Charter, to prepare what, in my view, was a model draft. I had drafted a similar agreement between South Africa and the Kingdom of Swaziland which came into force on 17 February 1982, the existence of which was made public in Pretoria after the conclusion of the Nkomati Accord on 31 March 1984.

I was amused to read that, in 1992, Chester Crocker in *High Noon in Southern Africa* wrote the following about the Nkomati Accord:

(B)ut Machel's and Botha's officials played a primary role in initiating the Nkomati Accord. Subtitled an 'agreement on non-aggression and good neighbourliness', this was a remarkable document. It literally and explicitly prohibited the parties from engaging in, or permitting the launch of, any form of armed attack on each other ... Nkomati was supposed to be the ultimate all-risk, no-loopholes insurance policy; it was drafted by deeply suspicious, traumatised minds on one side, and small-time lawyers on the other. Nothing would be left unspoken so that the other guy could come back and say, 'Oh, we never said we'd cut that out.'

In order to obtain iron-clad written commitments from Pretoria, Machel had signed the most comprehensive security agreement with South Africa in the region's history.

Significantly more or less accurate is the following:

By any measure, it was a great accomplishment for South Africa's diplomats and security bureaucrats, so eager for external recognition of its legitimate security interests against guerilla infiltration and terrorist violence.

Again more accurate is the following:

But Nkomati was hardly an isolated or unique agreement. Comparable arrangements, typically informal and secret, already existed to thwart ANC operations from or through Zimbabwe, Botswana, Lesotho, and Swaziland (the last accord was published after Nkomati).

Pik Botha took the draft to the next cabinet meeting where he got in-principle approval for it. It could not be openly resisted because the stated reason for South Africa's involvement in Mozambique, its assistance to the ANC, would fall away because it would become proscribed by the treaty.

The next meeting between South Africa and Mozambique was a plenary meeting in Maputo, the capital of Mozambique. The delegations were led by Pik Botha and Jacinto Veloso. The South African delegation included Magnus Malan, Minister of Defence, Louis le Grange, Minister of Law and Order, and Niel Barnard, head of the National Intelligence Service. The Mozambiquan delegation included Lieutenant Colonel F Honwana, a special assistant to President Machel (who later died in a plane crash with him), Colonel JO Monteiro, Minister of Justice, and Colonel S Vieira, Vice-Minister of Defence.

On the eve of the meeting, the South African Foreign Affairs component of the delegation stayed in the Foreign Affairs guesthouse. As was the custom, the preparatory meeting took place in the bar where monsieur Michel, the maître d'hôtel, introduced Pik Botha to grappa.

The following morning we went to Maputo in a chartered South African Airways Boeing. The 'lesser lights', as Pik Botha would refer to us, were sitting at the back of the plane. He summoned me to come and sit next to him and explain to him what the draft treaty involved, having confessed that he had not yet read it and that the grappa was taking its toll. Pik Botha had piloted the draft agreement through cabinet without having read it!

In Maputo the plenary meeting was held in the Mozambiquan Reserve Bank building – previously Barclays Bank. I remember standing on a balcony looking at the dilapidated city when one of the Mozambiquan delegates asked me whether I was admiring their beautiful city! The streets were dirty, the shops were empty and closed, and it was plain to see that Mozambique was in the grip of dreadful poverty. On their visits to South Africa, the Mozambiquan delegates would buy consumer items such as toothpaste, soap and shoe polish. We, on the other hand, would return from Mozambique with vast quantities of Mozambiquan prawns and Cuban cigars.

This being a plenary meeting, not much was achieved except in-principle agreements that the matters at hand should be taken forward.

The next plenary meeting took place in the Cape Sun hotel in Cape Town, not long after the meeting in Maputo.

As was his custom, Pik Botha was more interested in getting out a press release than in the nitty gritty. I drafted it, but the translation into Portuguese took so long that a helicopter trip around the peninsula had to be called off – which made Pik furious. I had to bear the brunt of his wrath, notwithstanding the fact that my job was completed in double-quick time.

That evening Pik Botha hosted a dinner in the Lady Anne Barnard room of the old Castle in Cape Town. Ray Killen, General Johan Coetzee and I were appointed to a drafting team of which the Mozambique members were, *inter alia*, Oscar Monteiro and Sergio Vieira. There was no representative of the South African Defence Force – no point in helping to draft a treaty they were, to begin with, opposed to.

We started working after dinner, and the brighter lights, i.e. Pik Botha and his ministerial counterpart and others, were in a separate room taking copious amounts of after-dinner drinks. It was painstaking and hard work, and my efforts were undermined by Coetzee's stupid attempts to be seen to make a contribution. I remember that there were two National Intelligence officers close by keeping a watch on matters. (The National Intelligence Service, under the leadership of Niel Barnard, was in favour of the agreement.)

At some point during the night, Pik enquired about our progress and Sergio Vieira went to tell him that I was delaying progress because of my knowledge of public international law, and that they had no such expert. Pik had enough savvy not to interfere, and suggested that Vieira go back to the negotiating table.

At three o'clock that morning I was the only person who had the full draft agreement. It was written by me on numerous pieces of paper.

Pik Botha decided that it was time for a speech, and he gleefully told the Mozambiquans how South Africa would shoot the hell out of them if they did not honour the agreement.

My work was not done yet. The Mozambiquans indicated that they wanted a typed copy of the agreement before they left at seven o'clock that morning. This meant that I had to go back to the office and dictate the entire agreement to a secretary. The Mozambiquans left that morning with a copy of what was later to be called, by Pik Botha, the Nkomati Accord.

The signing ceremony took place on 16 March 1984. It was a grand affair. It happened at the border town of Komatipoort. Large marquee tents were erected, and grand food and the best wines were served. It was quite a sight to see huge, fat Hercules and Boeing planes land on a gravel airstrip outside the town.

Before the ceremony took place, on a rugby field where PW Botha and Samora Machel made speeches, they met in a train coach which had been parked at the spot especially for the occasion.

This time the lesser lights had nothing to do.

For once South Africa had done something right, and it received a fair share of international approval for this. In the May 1984 edition of *South African Panorama*, a Foreign Affairs publication, there appeared an article which commenced as follows:

A new era of realism has dawned for Southern Africa with the signing of the non-aggression pact, the Accord of Nkomati, between the Republic of South Africa and the People's Republic of Mozambique, on the border between the two countries, on March 16, 1984. The accord is irrefutable proof that economic and geographic realities of Southern Africa, and a pragmatic approach to the region's problems, are of greater importance than widely divergent ideologies and antagonistic rhetoric. By placing their signatures on such a formal non-aggression pact in public, the President of the People's Republic of Mozambique, Samora Machel, and the Prime Minister of South Africa, Mr Pieter Willem Botha, *solemnly pledged to honour the clauses contained in the accord*' [my emphasis].

I later became the Chief State Law Adviser in the State President's Office, and was told by PW Botha himself that after the signing of the Nkomati Accord the Minister of Defence, General Magnus Malan, had asked permission for a last consignment of weapons to be delivered to Renamo notwithstanding the existence of the Nkomati Accord. Botha gave permission for this to be done.

In *The Other Side of History* Van Zyl Slabbert recounts how he congratulated Botha on the step away from regional aggression which the Nkomati Accord represented, and how, subsequently, it transpired that before, during and after the signing of the Nkomati Accord, South Africa continued to destabilise Mozambique.

I am vindicated in my seemingly lonely view that Constand Viljoen, the former chief of the South African Defence Force, is a much over-rated man by Van Zyl Slabbert's account of how he had asked Viljoen about speculation that South Africa was breaching the Nkomati Accord, only to be told that it was 'communist propaganda'.

Commenting on former defence minister Magnus Malan's book, *My lewe saam met die Suid-Afrikaanse Weermag* ('My life with the South African Defence Force'), Dr Leopold Scholtz, writing in *Die Burger*, warned his readers to approach the book with care, citing as one of many reasons the fact that Malan relates in passing how he had asked the air force to investigate rumours that unauthorised flights were undertaken to Mozambique in support of Renamo subsequent to the signing of the Nkomati Accord, and that the air force had denied this.

Once, *en route* to Lusaka with Pik Botha and Magnus Malan, the latter told me, while we were flying over Lake Kariba, that the South African Defence Force had contingency plans to sabotage it. To this day the sheer madness of it frightens the hell out of me.

One wonders what their supporters would have said if they had known that their esteemed leaders, the likes of PW Botha, Magnus Malan and Constand Viljoen, could not even honour their word, given, as it was, on behalf of their country.

Chester Crocker writes as follows with reference to Machel's disillusionment with Pretoria's commitment to the Nkomati Accord:

One moment, he (Machel) received contrite noises and pledges of tangible aid from top levels in Pretoria who were visibly scrambling to 'save Nkomati'; at the next, he was given fresh evidence of unauthorised flights and intensive unidentified radio transmissions emanating from across the eastern borders, from Malawi in the south to South Africa's Transvaal province. Anyone who knew the region knew that such activity could only have one source.

But it was hard for Machel to believe that this was all a co-herently organised act, authorised at the top. It looked more like one bunch of guys dashing around to cover for another. Machel may never have believed or understood the inner com-plexity behind South African ineptitude and deceit in its Mo-zambique policy. Indeed, it is hard to explain. How could the government in Pretoria have permitted one of its most strik-ing diplomatic accomplishments to be so promptly discredited? What purpose could be served, short term or long term, by act-ing to destroy what confidence existed in one's solemn word?

Solemn word indeed.

CHAPTER 4

MY APPOINTMENT AS
CHIEF STATE LAW ADVISER

Ironically, the events that led up to my appointment as Chief
State Law Adviser in the President's Office nearly saw me leaving the public service altogether.

In line with the government's policy of separate development, the territory of KwaZulu, in the province of Natal, at-
tained self-governing status with Chief Minister Buthelezi as
the head of government. The territory of KwaZulu included
land known as Ingwavuma, parts of which the Kingdom of
Swaziland wanted to incorporate into its territory because, so
it was alleged, the area is predominantly inhabited by Swazis.
The South African government accordingly resolved to excise
certain parts of Ingwavuma from the territory of KwaZulu as
a first step to transferring it to the Kingdom of Swaziland.

To achieve this, a task team was appointed which included
Roux Raath, the director-general at the time of the Department of Co-operation and Development (our euphemism for
black affairs), Advocate Daan Fölscher SC, Chief State Law
Adviser, Advocate William de Villiers SC, his junior advocate,
and me.

I remember that we met on a Saturday morning during
1982, and after much debate we concluded that the objective
of excising certain portions of Ingwavuma from the self-gov-

erning territory of KwaZulu could be achieved by a presidential proclamation.

During the course of the morning of the following Monday, a meeting took place under the chairmanship of the Prime Minister, PW Botha. It was also attended by Piet Koornhof, Minister of Co-operation and Development, Pik Botha, Roux Raath, Daan Fölscher, William de Villiers and me.

While PW Botha was being advised that he could excise the relevant portions of Ingwavuma from the territory of KwaZulu, I realised that the legal team had overlooked an aspect of the matter which would render the state president's proclamation unlawful. I gave Pik Botha a note to the effect that I had my reservations about the soundness of the advice that was being dispensed, and, as a result of his intervention, PW Botha asked me if I had anything to contribute to the debate. I said that I was no longer in agreement with the advice, and gave my reasons.

My advice was not followed, and I remember William de Villiers saying that, if the matter should go to court in Natal and the South African government lost there, it would be because the Natal bench was anti-government and that, in such eventuality, the matter should be appealed to the Appellate Division.

On 18 June 1982 the prime minister issued Proclamation R109 of 1982, the effect of which would have been, had it been valid, to excise portions of the district of Ingwavuma from KwaZulu.

Immediately after its publication, the government of Kwa-Zulu brought an application in the Durban and Coast local division of the Supreme Court against the national government

49

and the minister of Co-operation and Development in which it sought an order declaring that the Proclamation was null and void. On 25 June 1982 Judge Shearer issued a rule *nisi* calling upon the respondents to show cause why the proclamation should not be declared null and void, and why the minister of Co-operation and Development should not be interdicted from either assuming the administration of, or interfering with, the government of KwaZulu in the administration of the relevant portions of Ingwavuma. The rule was made returnable on 2 August 1982 but was extended, and to the best of my knowledge that matter was never finally disposed of.

On 28 June 1982 the prime minister tried again, this time by issuing Proclamation R121 of 1982 in which he relied on the provisions of Section 25(1) of the Black Administration Act, No. 38 of 1927, read with Section 21(1) of the Development Trust and Land Act, No. 18 of 1936, as well as Section 30(4) of the Self-governing Territories Constitution Act, No. 21 of 1971, in order to achieve the excision of Ingwavuma.

Again the validity of the proclamation was challenged, and a full bench of the Natal provincial division of the Supreme Court, comprising Deputy Judge President Milne and judges Van Heerden and Kriek, declared Proclamation R121 of 1982 null and void on the ground that it was not authorised by the statutory provisions on which the prime minister purported to rely when he issued it.

Another meeting, attended by the same persons as previously, convened under the chairmanship of PW Botha. Predictably he was advised that the decision had only gone against the government because the Natal bench was anti-government, and it was accordingly decided that the matter should be taken on appeal to the Appellate Division.

I was furious because I had advised the prime minister and his ministers, on the previous occasion, that they would lose the case. No-one referred to the fact that I had warned that the outcome was likely to be adverse to the government and that I too had taken the view that the proclamation would be unlawful.

Out of frustration I applied for a position as senior lecturer at the Rand Afrikaans University, and in due course was appointed to that position after having appeared before the vice chancellor, Professor Pieter de Lange, and other members of his academic staff.

However, I had severe reservations about my decision since I lectured part time at the University of Pretoria and the Rand Afrikaans University and, although I enjoyed it, I was not sure whether I would be satisfied doing that for the rest of my life. I decided not to take up the position, and to stay on as law adviser at the Department of Foreign Affairs.

In the event, the Ingwavuma matter was taken on appeal to the Appellate Division where four judges, with Chief Justice Rabie presiding, again ruled against the government.

PW Botha did not forget this incident and it was the main reason why, in 1984, following the commencement of the 1983 constitution, I was appointed to the position of Chief State Law Adviser in the State President's Office.

CHAPTER 5

MEETING MADIBA

Never in my life had I experienced a sense of being in the presence of a truly great person until I met Nelson Mandela. What follows is an account of how I came to meet him.

Following the adoption of the 1983 constitution, which commenced in 1984, a tricameral parliamentary system with an executive president was introduced. Previously the head of state, i.e. the state president, was a mere figurehead. Real power was vested in the prime minister and the cabinet, and, much like the queen, the state president was constitutionally obliged to give effect to the wishes of the prime minister and his cabinet.

That changed in 1984 when PW Botha became South Africa's first executive president and chair of the cabinet. Since the state president's powers were going to be vastly expanded as a result of the new dispensation, he needed more staff. One of the positions that was created in his office was that of Chief State Law Adviser.

I applied for this position and was appointed to it – largely, I believe, because of the facts I have related in the previous chapter. This was a senior position, the equivalent of a deputy director-general of a state department.

During the 1980s South Africa became progressively more isolated in the international community, and its traditional Western 'friends' came under increased pressure to do something about the situation in South and southern Africa.

To this end the Commonwealth nations appointed what was known as the Eminent Persons Group ('EPG'), a small committee headed by former Australian prime minister Fraser and General Obasanjo, formerly (and currently) the president of Nigeria. During 1985 this group visited South Africa and other countries in southern Africa to negotiate with various leaders, organisations and other people of their choice.

Not surprisingly, the EPG requested the South African government to be allowed to meet with Nelson Mandela. This request was granted, provided that one South African official could attend the meeting. So it came about that PW Botha designated me to attend the EPG's meeting with Nelson Mandela in the Pollsmoor Prison at Tokai near Cape Town.

The meeting was held early one morning, and it was then that I met the man popularly known as Madiba. I had decided beforehand that I was not going to participate in the discussion, and to restrict my role to that of an observer only. That, however, was not Mandela's thinking.

I was utterly amazed by the intellectual skill, acumen and charm with which he engaged the EPG, and by the knowledge which he displayed in doing so.

By then the EPG had formulated a negotiating concept involving the cessation of violence as a prelude to the unbanning of the ANC (and other banned organisations) and the release of Mandela and other political prisoners – its 'matching commitments' formula. Throughout the conversation Mandela, seemingly innocently, tried to involve me. I remember, for example, that after having said that Professor Tom Lodge of the University of the Witwatersrand was probably the foremost South African expert on communism, he stated that he was sure that I would agree with that observation. Although I did agree, I said nothing.

The EPG proceeded to put its proposal to Mandela, and he responded positively to it. Then, totally in command of the conversation and the situation, he turned to me and asked me whether there was anything I wanted to say. Instead of simply keeping quiet, I asked whether his response to the EPG proposal implied that if the South African government accepted the proposal, the ANC would follow suit. He responded quick as a flash: 'No, Dr Heunis, the ANC accepts the proposal whether or not the South African government does!'

In one sentence he had occupied the moral high ground, and in the process had presented the ANC as being a reasonable organisation willing to compromise in order to achieve peace in South and southern Africa. The ball was squarely in the government's court.

During a tea break he singled me out for some small talk, and animatedly spoke about the skills of my cousin, the South African rugby fullback, Johan Heunis. I was asked to convey his regards and admiration to Johan. I was exposed to Mandela's legendary charm at its best.

During the second session of the meeting he tried the same trick and attempted to involve me in the discussions again. This time I was ready to retaliate with the following: 'I don't make the same mistake twice, Dr Mandela.' There was spontaneous laughter all round, and I think he was flattered by the fact that I had implicitly acknowledged that he had successfully tricked me on the previous occasion.

I left that meeting filled with admiration for a man who was

presented by the powers that be as South Africa's most danger-
ous enemy. By then I had read a lot about Mandela, including
his speech at the conclusion of the Rivonia trial at which he
and others were convicted on charges of treason. That speech
had all the hallmarks of a truly extraordinary author.

Naturally the Department of Correctional Services had attempted to record what was said at the EPG meeting. I say
'attempted' because it was a dismal failure and, being the only
government representative present, I was called upon to provide feedback as to what had transpired.

I told PW Botha that he simply had to meet Mandela. His
response was that Mandela's status (that of a prisoner) would
first have to change. In the end he met Mandela without such
a change in status having taken place, and shortly before he
was ousted as president.

I could not understand this at all since, as recounted elsewhere, PW Botha himself had allowed Kobie Coetsee, the
Minister of Correctional Services, to meet Mandela.

Following my resignation as Chief State Law Adviser in the
Office of the State President, I was told by Daan Prinsloo and
Jack Viviers, two officials in PW Botha's office who were very
close to Botha (Prinsloo subsequently wrote his official biography), that Botha had decided that I would negotiate with
Mandela on behalf of the South African government while he
was still in prison. This task was subsequently performed by
the head of the National Intelligence Service, Dr Niel Barnard. In a later chapter I relate how I came to lose what must
surely have been the most challenging and exciting responsibility imaginable for a public servant – negotiating with Mandela.

Following the commencement of the new political dispen-sation, by which time I had resigned from the State President's Office and was in private practice in Cape Town, I represented Mandela, in his official capacity, in the Constitutional Court.

The nature of the man is best illustrated by the following. On the evening of 14 October 1997 I arrived at my home at about eight o'clock. Mandela was then president. As I pulled into the garage, my children came running out shouting that I should come inside quickly because the President wanted to speak to me on the telephone.

It was indeed Madiba, who told me that he had just signed the letters patent in which he appointed me as senior counsel and that he wanted to congratulate me in person.

CHAPTER 6

SIDELINING THE
SPECIAL CABINET COMMITTEE

In the previous chapter, I related that PW Botha had decided that I should be responsible for negotiating with Nelson Mandela. There were other indications that PW Botha wanted me to play a more important role in his office than simply being his law adviser.

During July 1986 Botha had a critically important meeting with Sir Geoffrey Howe, the British Foreign Minister, who had to take up the Eminent Persons Group's concept of matching commitments on violence between the South African government and the ANC. I was the only official present.

PW Botha had gone to a lot of trouble to prepare for this meeting, and bombarded Howe with an account of his government's achievements as far as the economic upliftment of the country's people was concerned, as well as reform measures that had been taken. He lectured Howe about this for a long time. Howe was clearly taken aback, and tried to convey to Botha that none of those facts were in issue, but that the situation in South Africa was deteriorating by the day and that an internationally acceptable solution to South Africa's political problems had become imperative.

Predictably, Botha lost his temper and left Howe in no doubt that the South African government would not be dictated to and would act in accordance with its own insights as to what was in the best interests of the country.

The meeting with Howe in Pretoria was followed by one in Cape Town with Herman Nickel, the United States ambassador to South Africa at the time. Again I was the only official present at the meeting. On this occasion Botha actually said that South Africa would go to war rather than be dictated to. Realising that he had just mooted the possibility of war with the United States, he feebly continued by saying that naturally South Africa did not want war. I was acutely embarrassed by this performance, and Nickel, like Howe, was quite taken aback.

I interpose to remark that Botha seemingly had no sense of the importance of these two meetings.

In Europe Margaret Thatcher was resisting the imposition of Commonwealth measures against South Africa, and in the United States Ronald Reagan was doing the same in respect of domestic sanctions.

Following Botha's disastrous meeting with Howe, Thatcher had no choice but to give ground at a Commonwealth mini-summit. On 5 August a majority at the mini-summit endorsed a sweeping list of voluntary economic and other sanctions ranging from visa, tourism and air links to bans on new investments and loans and imports of South African agricultural goods, coal, uranium, iron and steel.

In *High Noon in Southern Africa*, Chester Crocker recounts that by 24 July Nancy Kassebaum, the Republican chairperson of the Africa subcommittee of the US Senate Foreign Relations Committee, who knew that Reagan had to 'get out front' on the South African issue or lose the support of the Republican majority in the Senate on the issue, had introduced a bill to prohibit any new investments in South Africa. Senate majority leader Bob Dole called on the floor of the Senate for the appointment of a presidential emissary to swing into action. Dick Lugar, Senate Foreign Relations Committee chairman, had already begun publicly to modify his stance on sanctions legislation, moving from a position where he favoured legislation that would threaten future sanctions to a two-phase approach calling for immediate application of certain measures and the adoption of others within 18 to 24 months unless significant progress occurred in ending apartheid. He circulated the outline of proposed legislation, including items such as air links and visa restrictions as well as trade bans on certain products from South Africa's parastatal companies such as Iscor.

Crocker also recounts that by 29 July, following Botha's insult of Howe, beefing up of the Lugar legislation began and it soon saw amendments on the Senate floor, by narrow majorities, to include a broad range of high-sounding but patently protectionist import bans borrowed from the Commonwealth list of measures that Thatcher was resisting in London.

Following the 5 August Commonwealth mini-summit's endorsement of the list of voluntary economic and other sanctions, the US Senate on 15 August voted 84 to 14 for a sanctions bill, seeing Reagan carrying only 25% of his own party. The bill would end landing rights, ban investments and new public and private sector loans, prohibit petroleum exports, and ban imports of agricultural and fisheries products, coal, uranium, textile products, iron and steel.

On 12 September the House of Representatives passed the Senate sanctions bill by 308 to 77 votes. On 26 September Reagan vetoed the bill, a veto that was overridden by the House of Representatives on the same day by a vote of 313 to 83. On 2 October the Senate overrode the Reagan veto by a vote of 78 to 21.

All this against the backdrop of what Crocker refers to as the 'haemorrhaging of the President's constitutional authority and foreign affairs' which 'would only get worse if he lost (the) battle'.

Be that as it may, it was because of my resignation as Chief State Law Adviser that Niel Barnard, the head of the National Intelligence Service and a good friend of mine, was instructed by Botha to commence talks with Mandela whilst the latter was still in prison. In my view it was quite inappropriate to have charged Barnard with this responsibility, as it would have been inappropriate so to charge me. We were both public servants, and the issues involving Mandela, his release and the unbanning of the ANC were decidedly political. Also, by then the Special Cabinet Committee chaired by my father in his capacity as Minister of Constitutional Development and Planning, which had been appointed to grapple with the issue of black political rights, had not been able to make meaningful progress.

The committee also comprised the Minister of Foreign Affairs, Pik Botha, the Minister of Education and Training, Gerrit Viljoen (charged with responsibility for the education of black South Africans in 'white' areas), the Minister of Law and Order, Louis le Grange, the Minister of Education and the Transvaal Leader of the National Party, FW de Klerk, and the Minister of Justice and Correctional Services, Kobie Coetsee.

My father, Pik Botha and Gerrit Viljoen were regarded as enlightened nationalists, whereas the latter three were regarded as conservative. Significantly, Daan Prinsloo of the State President's Office, a confidant of PW Botha, attended meetings of this committee.

In his autobiography *The Last Trek – A New Beginning*, FW de Klerk says that the committee became the main forum for debate within the government on key constitutional questions, and that its activities very soon became just as important to him as his cabinet portfolio, his chairmanship of the Minister's Council of the 'white' House of Assembly, and his leadership of the National Party in the Transvaal.

The obvious choice to conduct negotiations with Mandela would have been my father or, for that matter, the entire committee. In fact, my father had indicated on a number of occasions that he wanted to meet Mandela, but Kobie Coetsee would not allow it. This is truly amazing. The fact that Kobie Coetsee was the Minister of Correctional Services did not mean that Mandela became his property. Mandela was a key role player and the key to a negotiated settlement of the South African political issues. The fact that the Minister of Constitutional Development, having expressed a desire to speak with Mandela, was not allowed to do so because the Minister of Correctional Services did not approve of it, is mind-boggling, particularly if one bears in mind that a public official, accountable to PW Botha, was allowed to see Mandela.

Amongst my father's personal documents which are being kept at the Institute of Contemporary History in Bloemfontein, there are copies of two letters that he wrote to PW Botha and copied to Kobie Coetsee, one of October 1984 and one of January 1985. In both of them he requested to be allowed to meet with Mandela. Neither seems to have been responded to, and it is a fact that he never met Mandela while the latter was in prison.

Barnard's meetings with Mandela yielded nothing concrete during Botha's reign, nor could they, because he could not negotiate with Mandela on a political level with a political mandate. Predictably the conversations with Mandela were bugged, and, presumably, the transcripts provided good bedtime reading for Botha. While no progress was made regarding the resolution of the burning issue of black political aspirations, the country was in a state of emergency and virtual civil war.

One incident graphically illustrates the futility of PW Botha's virtual inaction at the time. In his opening speech to parliament at the beginning of 1985 Botha offered to release Mandela on condition that he undertook to renounce violence. Mandela's emphatic rejection of this offer was made public by his daughter, Zinzi.

At some point thereafter the Department of Foreign Affairs prepared a letter to Margaret Thatcher for Botha's signature in which the phrase 'suspension of violence' was used. In her response the British prime minister obviously latched onto the shift from 'renunciation' of violence to 'suspension' of violence. Botha, who did not intend any shift in position, phoned me to ask what 'suspension' meant and I had to explain to him that it had a temporary connotation, and that it did not mean the same as a renunciation or a cessation of violence. He was very angry with the Department of Foreign Affairs for having put him in this predicament, and a letter in which he set out the correct position had to be sent to Thatcher.

Her response was particularly vicious, as I discovered one Sunday afternoon when I was summoned to the Presidency in Pretoria where PW Botha and Pik Botha, both inspired by copious amounts of Scotch, were overseeing attempts of members of Pik's first team (to the best of my recollection Les Manley and Herbert Beukes were there) to prepare a response to Thatcher's letter. I was drafted in to assist with this attempt. In the end we were able to draft a letter which had the effect of defusing the tense situation between the two heads of government, but none of this was to any avail, given what was at stake in South Africa.

In his autobiography FW de Kerk recounts how my father tried, unsuccessfully, to exert pressure on PW Botha with regard to Mandela's release from prison, and continues to state the following: 'Despite his position as Minister of Constitutional Development and my position as leader of the National Party in the Transvaal, neither Heunis nor I was informed at that stage of the exploratory discussions with Mandela which were being conducted by a few senior officials and Minister Kobie Coetsee.'

Judging by photographs that have now been published, *inter alia* in *Mandela, the Authorised Portrait*, taken while Mandela was still in prison, the people who had discussions with him were Kobie Coetsee himself, Niel Barnard, Fanie van der Merwe, at the time Director-General of the Department of Justice, and General Willemse, the head of the Department of Correctional Services.

Predictably these talks yielded nothing of substance since the public officials could not have had a mandate involving meaningful discussions, and Kobie Coetsee, apart from not being the responsible minister, was certainly not up to the challenge. He was a dull, uncertain and conservative member of

Botha's cabinet, and a very reluctant participant in the negotiations which led to the commencement of the new constitutional dispensation.

While my father's frustration at not being able to make
progress with negotiations regarding black political aspirations,
and because he was only able to talk with non-representative
leaders, was reaching boiling point, these men were talking
to Mandela without his knowledge and notwithstanding frequent requests for him to be allowed to talk to Mandela.

It will also be recalled that I mentioned that I had recom-
mended to PW Botha that he should meet with Mandela, but
that he responded that he could not do so before Mandela's
status had changed. Presumably that meant that he could not
meet Mandela while the latter was still in prison. This notwithstanding, he allowed Kobie Coetsee to meet with Mandela and, in the final analysis, himself met with Mandela shortly
before he was forced to resign, in what was no doubt an attempt to steal a march on FW de Klerk. By all accounts it was
an inconsequential meeting that will probably be remembered
largely because of the subsequent fall-out between Botha and
Barnard because the latter had elected to destroy the recording that was made of the meeting. It had no historical significance!

In a recent letter to *Die Burger*, a Cape Town-based Afrikaans
newspaper, Maritz Spaarwater, formerly a chief director in the
National Intelligence Service and a friend of mine, wrote that
the State Security Council took a decision in August 1989 that
the possibility of officially entering into negotiations with the
ANC had to be investigated. The National Intelligence Service was mandated to do this investigation. A surer sign of PW

Botha's mindset and the state of the nation is difficult to imagine. By then my father had resigned from politics.

According to Spaarwater the resolution was carefully and deliberately worded ambiguously to avoid the resistance of the 'conservatives' in the cabinet, then under the leadership of FW de Klerk. This approach had allegedly been promoted with PW Botha by Kobie Coetsee and a number of top officials, no doubt Van der Merwe and Barnard. Botha supported it fully.

I know for a fact that PW Botha never intended to accommodate black political aspirations in a single constitutional dispensation; he would certainly have scoffed at a suggestion that the so-called independent states, i.e. Transkei, Bophuthatswana, Venda and Ciskei, be re-incorporated into the Republic of South Africa.

Spaarwater's suggestion, albeit made by implication, that Kobie Coetsee was an enlightened member of Botha's cabinet, is misleading as evidenced by his destructive and recalcitrant approach to the negotiation process described elsewhere.

According to Spaarwater, senior officials of the National Intelligence Service under the leadership of Mike Louw, then the deputy director-general of the service, met with the leadership of the ANC in the persons of Thabo Mbeki and Jacob Zuma, in Switzerland later that month, as a consequence of the State Security Council decision.

In *The Other Side of History* Van Zyl Slabbert also mentions that towards the end of the PW Botha era contact was made between the governing establishment represented by Kobie Coetsee, Niel Barnard and Professor Willie Esterhuyse, on the one hand, and Mandela and ANC exiles such as Mbeki on the other hand. Subsequent to the publication of Van Zyl

Slabbert's book, he and Willie Esterhuyse engaged in a debate in *Die Burger*. According to one of Esterhuyse's letters, he arranged the first meeting, which took place on 12 September 1989, on 31 May 1989 at the request of the National Intelligence Service. He also related that Niel Barnard had met with Mandela more than forty times, and confirmed that FW de Klerk was only informed of the talks with the government in exile on 16 September 1989.

In a subsequent letter Esterhuyse revealed that the decision referred to by Spaarwater as ambiguous was taken by the State Security Council on 16 August 1989, a day after De Klerk was sworn in as acting president, in which capacity he was, on that day, the chairman of the State Security Council. Both Spaarwater and Esterhuyse referred to the fact that when he was told of the negotiations, De Klerk was at first upset about it, but, 'in the true spirit of a great leader', subsequently 'picked up the ball and ran with it'. Hindsight has always been an exact science. The fact of the matter is that the resolution was so ambiguous that De Klerk did not realise that negotiations with the ANC were being mandated.

Ironically, when officials of the Department of Constitutional Development, to wit Fanie Cloete and Kobus Jordaan, attempted to make contact with the ANC during my father's term as minister, their security clearance was withdrawn. In this regard Fanie Cloete wrote in an article in *Die Burger* of 16 February 2006, styled 'Chris Heunis and the erosion of apartheid', that the fear of political demise gave the conservative die-hards, backed by the security forces, the upper hand and resulted in PW Botha turning against my father, and in 1987 he was deliberately excluded from all negotiations with Mandela.

A few days after publication of the Spaarwater letter, Dave Steward, executive director of the FW de Klerk Foundation, responded to Spaarwater's letter. According to Steward's letter, De Klerk and other senior members of the cabinet were simply not informed about discussions with Mandela. In his letter he pointed out that Spaarwater openly acknowledged that the National Intelligence Service deliberately attempted to keep senior cabinet members in the dark by the ambiguous wording of the State Security Council resolution regarding the possibility of negotiations with the ANC. De Klerk himself, the Transvaal leader of the National Party and chairman of the Minister's Council in the House of Assembly, was not informed about the contact with Mandela before he was elected as leader of the National Party in February 1989.

What is patently clear is that PW Botha undermined the work of the Special Cabinet Committee under my father's chairmanship which was responsible for devising a political dispensation which would have seen full participation in the political process by all South Africans, by entrusting securocrats under his control with negotiations with the ANC and keeping his (enlightened) political colleagues in the dark.

The point about this is that although the purpose of the original Spaarwater letter was to call for the necessary recognition for PW Botha, saying that but for the traditional greatest fear of National Party leaders, namely splitting the party, Botha would probably have moved faster and that the same conservative pressure was the cause of the stepping back evidenced by his earlier Rubicon speech, Botha effectively sidelined the forces for reform in his cabinet.

As I recount elsewhere, the latter observation about the

Rubicon speech is simply not correct. As far as the first one is concerned, I know that PW Botha would not have taken any ground-breaking steps as far as the political aspirations of black people were concerned.

I base this view on the simple fact that he once told me, in plain terms, that he did not like black people, illustrating his point by saying of Reddy, the leader of the Solidarity Party in the Indian House of Delegates, that although he was a nice person, he was too black for Botha's liking!

CHAPTER 7

FREDERIK VAN ZYL SLABBERT

Dr Frederik van Zyl Slabbert, a well-known and widely respected South African sociologist and former leader of the Progressive Federal Party, is another politician for whom I have the utmost respect.

It is customary for senior officials doing parliamentary service to sit in a specially allocated bench when their ministers participate in parliamentary debates. This I had to do both as law adviser to the Department of Foreign Affairs when Pik Botha was due to participate in a debate, as well as when I was Chief State Law Adviser in the State President's Office when he was due to participate in any debate. I therefore had frequent opportunity to listen to Slabbert's parliamentary speeches which were always well prepared, insightful and delivered with style and dignity. I recall doing the uncustomary thing of sending him notes congratulating him on his speeches, much to the dismay of some of my colleagues.

Traditionally parliament's business commenced each year with the customary no-confidence debate. It was during such a debate, on 11 February 1986, that Slabbert, to the utter amazement of the entire country, including his parliamentary colleagues, announced his resignation as leader of the Progressive Federal Party and member of parliament.

His position was that parliament had become irrelevant to

the broader political scene in South Africa, a position which he *inter alia* based on a conversation which he had had with State President PW Botha the previous year, and which Botha taped without his knowledge. Significantly Slabbert himself describes the dramatic and calculated breaches of the Nkomati Accord as the final straw.

Instead of earnestly reflecting upon the reasons advanced by Slabbert for his resignation, Botha, in typical knee-jerk style, decided to release a transcript of the recording to disprove Slabbert's claim that he realised, at the meeting with Botha, that he was wasting his time. At that meeting, Slabbert *inter alia* pleaded with Botha to release Mandela unconditionally. Botha smiled and told Slabbert that the majority of black people supported him, Botha!

I considered it wholly inappropriate that the meeting had been recorded, and equally inappropriate for the state president to have wanted to make known the contents of what had been said at that meeting.

Be that as it may, I remember that a few ministers, including Kobie Coetsee, the Minister of Justice, assembled in my office in Tuynhuys after a cabinet meeting to discuss the issue. Kobie Coetsee took the view that Slabbert probably had copyright in the recording and it was decided that I should call him and ask his permission for its contents to be made public.

To this day I regret having carried out that instruction. I traced Slabbert to his in-laws' farm in Swaziland, stated the purpose of my call, and duly received permission from him for the contents of the tape to be made public. There were no qualifications. It was a shameful way to treat one of South Africa's finest sons. In the event, the transcript of the tape recording did not disprove anything that Slabbert had said in his resignation speech – on the contrary. His book, *The Other Side of History*, also served as an inspiration for me to complete my own effort mainly because I was able to corroborate many of the facts and perceptions put forward by him.

Years later, when I was practising as senior counsel at the Cape bar, I represented the former head of the National Intelligence Service, Niel Barnard, in a defamation suit against Ebrahim Rasool, then the leader of the ANC opposition in the provincial legislature, and subsequently the premier.

Although Slabbert did not see eye to eye with Barnard on political matters, he held him in high regard and immediately consented to be a character witness when I asked him whether he would testify on Barnard's behalf. This is indicative of the nature of the man. He would certainly have picked up a lot of flack for giving evidence on behalf of the apartheid regime's chief spy, but had no hesitation in agreeing to my request for the simple reason that he considered it the right thing to do.

CHAPTER 8

THE POLICE'S SECRET FUND

It is related elsewhere that in 1984 South Africa was given a tricameral parliamentary system in which whites were represented in the House of Assembly, Coloureds in the House of Representatives, and Indians in the House of Delegates. Blacks were excluded.

In the event of a deadlock between any of these components of parliament in the process of making legislation, the matter would be referred by the state president to the President's Council, in which the majority party in the House of Assembly had an in-built majority, for resolution.

The first legislation referred to the President's Council for the purpose of deadlock-breaking was Law and Order minister Louis le Grange's draft legislation which provided for a secret account for the South African Police.

The Labour Party, the majority party in the House of Representatives, was opposed to the draft bill. PW Botha decided that it should be referred to the President's Council for resolution. Since I was his law adviser, I was on legitimate terrain when I strongly advised him against this. I had two strings to my bow. The first was that the tricameral parliamentary system had very limited credibility, which would be further undermined by an early invocation of the deadlock-breaking capacity of the National Party-loaded President's Council.

The second was that there was no reason for the South African Police to have a secret account. Certainly, I was not convinced of that and, to his credit, I did not believe that PW Botha was. The reasons furnished in support of the establishment of such a secret account were pathetically unconvincing and inadequate.

Following my advice, Botha stemmed the tide for the time being by instructing that I should meet with Kobie Coetsee, the Minister of Justice, and Louis le Grange, the Minister of Law and Order, in an attempt to persuade the latter not to pursue the bill – a very unusual brief for a public servant.

With the assistance of a very good friend of mine in the Department of Justice, who was then its parliamentary officer, Deon Rudman (he subsequently became a deputy director-general of the Department of Justice), we stopped the progress of the bill on the authority only of the fact that PW Botha had told me that he would want both ministers to talk to me before any further steps were taken. I should mention that at that time the two ministers were at loggerheads to the extent that they hardly spoke to each other.

Coetsee knew about PW Botha's instructions; Le Grange did not. Botha had assured me that he would tell Le Grange of his instructions at a meeting that they had scheduled for the very afternoon on which I was given the go-ahead to attempt to stop referral of the bill to the President's Council.

Botha must have forgotten to tell Le Grange about the arrangement, because when he found out that there had been an intervention which resulted in the progress of the bill being stopped, he called a meeting of senior officials of his department at which he required my attendance. At the meeting he was armed with my memorandum to PW Botha in which I motivated why I thought that the bill was unnecessary and unwise. Frequent sarcastic references to the memorandum followed, and I remember interrupting him, while he was reading from it, to point out to him when statements were made in inverted commas. My father later told me that Le Grange had subsequently confided in him that he saw that I had lost my temper. My capacity to live with the beast was wearing thin. In the event I lost, again.

Le Grange insisted that the police needed the bill and there was never any discussion, as foreshadowed by PW Botha, between the two ministers, and I never had an occasion to try and convince them that the bill was not necessary and, more importantly, that referral to the President's Council would be undermining the credibility of the tricameral parliamentary system, such as it was. Unsurprisingly PW Botha decided to refer the dispute to the President's Council. Predictably it sanctioned the progress of the bill, and it subsequently became law.

That law created the fund from which, *inter alia*, Vlakplaas, the headquarters of scandalous clandestine police activity, was paid for.

CHAPTER 9

PW BOTHA'S RUBICON

Viewed from one perspective, PW Botha's infamous Rubicon speech at the Natal congress of the National Party on 15 August 1985 was a personal and national disaster. Viewed from another perspective, it can be seen as an important turning point in South Africa's political history inasmuch as Western governments, which still resisted sanctions against South Africa, finally lost faith in Botha's capacity to bring about meaningful reform in South Africa. This in turn led to pressure from the entire international community, most importantly the Western countries, which finally persuaded FW de Klerk to release Nelson Mandela and others, unban the ANC, and engage in negotiations which resulted in a fully democratic South Africa.

It was widely expected that PW Botha would use the occasion to make important announcements about constitutional reform which would, at the very least, have begun to address the fact that blacks were excluded from government at national level.

According to an article published on 15 August 2005 in *Die Burger*, an Afrikaans daily newspaper which circulates in the Western Cape, Pik Botha, South Africa's foreign minister at the time, opined that it remained a mystery why PW Botha did not make the announcements which everyone thought he would. Pik Botha is quoted as having said that as a 'tip to

PW Botha' he prepared a draft speech of six to eight pages in which the most important elements of the dismantling of apartheid were contained. According to FW de Klerk's autobiography, *The Last Trek – A New Beginning*, that contribution was in fact compiled by Carl von Hirschberg, a deputy director-general in the Department of Foreign Affairs at the time. This is confirmed in PW Botha's (authorised) biography *Stem uit die Wilderness* ('A voice from the Wilderness'), by Daan Prinsloo. PW Botha gave Pik Botha 'the impression' that his proposals were acceptable and on the basis thereof he marketed the speech in Europe. More recently, following PW Botha's death, there was again much speculation as to why he did not deliver the speech he was widely expected to deliver.

What follows is the true account of the reason for the Rubicon disaster.

At the time my father was the Minister of Constitutional Development and Planning, and chairperson of the Special Cabinet Committee which had to look into the question of a constitutional framework able to accommodate the political aspirations of black South Africans. He was frustrated because the Committee made little progress with negotiations with blacks because their real leaders were in jail and they were not represented in government at national level. The leaders of the homelands, with the exception of Chief Buthelezi, had no credibility and could not, in any event, negotiate on behalf of black people who were living in South Africa.

My father then wrote a letter to PW Botha to say that he was not making any progress, and made certain proposals to take matters forward. PW Botha reacted by saying that he would convene a meeting of the cabinet, deputy ministers (who were not members of the cabinet) and the chairpersons of the President's Council's committees at the Military Intelligence College in a converted observatory in Pretoria. The meeting took place on 2 August 1985. Botha was due to address the Natal National Party congress on 15 August 1985.

My father addressed the meeting, a debate followed, and it was *inter alia* decided that black people would be accommodated in the cabinet as an interim measure pending the outcome of negotiations with black South Africans to reach agreement on their accommodation in a new constitutional dispensation.

This was particularly significant because it recognised the fact that blacks would inevitably have had to be accommodated at central government level in South Africa, and that the homelands were no answer to blacks' political aspirations. The homelands were relatively small (unconsolidated) geographic entities within the boundaries of the Republic of South Africa where various black ethnic groups were allowed to 'govern' themselves and ultimately attain 'independence'. It also recognised that blacks were part and parcel of the South African citizenry, and accordingly entitled to participate in the governance of the country at national level.

FW de Klerk's recollection, as set out in his autobiography, is that Botha asked cabinet members to suggest ideas for the speech he was due to deliver on 15 August. According to him, my father drafted extensive suggestions which he sent to the President, as did the Department of Foreign Affairs. Also, the Department of Foreign Affairs had been authorised to brief leading Western governments on the speech and to urge them to respond with messages of encouragement and support. To this end Pik Botha went on a special mission to Europe, where he met senior representatives of various governments and informed them of the new direction that he expected PW Botha to announce.

According to Chester Crocker's *High Noon in Southern Africa*, Pik Botha suggested an urgent meeting to discuss the road ahead as early as 2 August. In the event, Botha met American State Department officials in Vienna on 8 August where, according to Crocker, he

> was at his thespian best …, walking out on limbs far beyond the zone of safety to persuade us that his president was on the verge of momentous announcements. We learned of plans for bold reform steps, new formulas on constitutional moves, and further thinking relative to the release of Mandela.

After the adjournment of the meeting, PW Botha asked my father whether he would prepare a draft speech for him, based on the decisions that had been taken, so that he could announce them at the opening of the Natal Congress of the National Party the following weekend. My father and the director-general of his department at the time, Prof. Andreas van Wyk, formerly dean of the faculty of law of the University of Stellenbosch and subsequently vice chancellor and rector of that university, together with other senior officials spent that Friday drafting the speech itself since my father had promised that he would take it to PW Botha's residence before one o'clock the following Saturday.

While driving to PW Botha's official residence on the Saturday morning, he saw *Argus* posters which revealed that the essence of the speech had been disclosed to the media. When my father got to PW Botha's official residence, Botha was waiting for him on the *stoep*. He was angry as hell, and took the speech without any explanation and without inviting my father in.

That evening PW Botha phoned my father to tell him that he had no intention of delivering the 'Prog' (at the time considered to be the liberal white element in the South African parliament) speech which my father had prepared. My father told him that it was not a Prog speech, and that it simply reflected the decisions which had been taken at the Military Intelligence College, and the conversation ended there. PW Botha then phoned all his ministers and told them that he wanted to see them in the cabinet room in Pretoria the following Monday. He arrived with the speech which he ultimately delivered, and read it to the cabinet ministers, who had to listen as if they were Grade 1 learners. When he was finished, my father was the only one who spoke. He said that he had given Botha a draft which, in his view, reflected what had been decided and that he had no further comments.

That is how it came about that Botha delivered a speech which Sampie Terreblanche described in *Die Burger* as 'a quickening of history', and which *inter alia* led Chase Manhattan Bank, followed by other international banks, to suspend loans to South Africa.

According to the 15 August *Die Burger* article Professor Anton van Niekerk, a well-known Stellenbosch professor of philosophy, described it as one of the greatest opportunities ever missed.

PW Botha's biography, *Stem uit die Wilderness* ('A voice from the Wilderness'), was written by Dr Daan Prinsloo, a political scientist who, during Botha's time as state president, was attached to the President's Office where one of his main responsibilities was to write speeches for Botha. He wrote the Botha biography while still in the public service, in line with a cabinet decision, initiated by Botha, that the government would sponsor the biographies of retired state presidents. Against the factual backdrop of what actually happened, as far as my father's involvement is concerned, it is fascinating to see what Prinsloo has to say. What follows is his account.

At the end of the Military Intelligence College meeting, Botha requested the Special Cabinet Committee to make recommendations to him with a view to his opening speech of the National Party Natal congress (no mention being made of the fact that Botha had asked my father to prepare a draft speech reflecting what had been decided).

Following the meeting, my father furnished Botha with a draft contribution to the speech which had been prepared in conjunction with other members of the Special Cabinet Committee, which Botha used in part. (My father and Andreas van Wyk, with the assistance of other senior officials, prepared a draft speech, not a contribution. No other ministers were involved.) Together with De Klerk and other members of the Special Cabinet Committee, my father also prepared a redrafted Program of Principles of the National Party. Barend du Plessis presented an input concerning the economy which was, for the most part, used by Botha, and Pik Botha made Carl von Hirchsberg's contribution available to Botha. Finally, Botha also had short contributions which had been prepared by his own office.

According to Prinsloo, Botha started preparing his speech in phases and, while he was busy doing that, the first speculative reports appeared in the local media. According to him, the last straw was a report which appeared in the *Weekend Argus* which referred to the possibility of blacks in the President's Council and the cabinet, and which concluded as follows:

> Full details have not yet been worked out, but President Botha will start spelling them out at the national congress of the National Party next weekend. ... Nationalist politicians ... say that the government is trying to find a power-sharing formula with blacks without stating this too openly for fear of a right-wing backlash.

Thereupon Botha phoned my father and told him that he was definitely not going to make that sort of announcement in his speech, that he would not be forced in a direction by speculation, and that, in view of 'that sort' of report, he would give his own content to the speech. (No mention is made of Botha's conduct when he received the draft speech, and none of him referring to it as a 'Prog' speech.)

According to Prinsloo, the *Weekend Argus* report was written by Tos Wentzel, who had based the report on information obtained from someone who previously had good contacts with the Department of Constitutional Development and Planning. Prinsloo regards the *Weekend Argus* report as an important catalyst which resulted in the fact that the Rubicon speech of 15 August was totally different from what the members of the Special Cabinet Committee had planned and hoped for, and what had been envisaged by local and international expectation. (In fact, Botha's pettiness and volatile temperament were the catalysts.)

The point about this is, of course, that the Rubicon speech was supposed to reflect what had been decided at the Military Intelligence College meeting, and it is clear that Botha unilaterally decided to deviate from those decisions because he was angry about the fact that, as he perceived it, his thunder had been stolen as a consequence of speculative newspaper reporting – as if that could have been prevented, given the fact that Pik Botha had been sent overseas to invite positive reaction to the speech.

Interestingly, Prinsloo's rendition contains no reference to the meeting which Botha had convened for the Monday. According to him, Botha read his speech to the National Party members of the cabinet subsequent to its formal Wednesday meeting, where it was listened to by the assembled ministers without objection or opposition. Pik Botha was supposed to have said, according to PW Botha, that it was a speech which he could live with.

I prefer my father's recollection also because, according to Prinsloo himself, subsequent to the meeting at which Botha read his speech to his cabinet colleagues, my father made attempts to rescue the situation, but to no avail. If Botha had only read the speech on the Wednesday, there would not have been time for such rescue attempts as there might have been and which Prinsloo himself refers to.

On 14 August 1985, a day before the Rubicon disaster, my father prepared a speech for an Elite Leaders' Conference at Stellenbosch. On 16 August, the day after the Rubicon debacle, he made a note on the speech to the effect that it should not be released, and prepared a new speech.

If he had delivered the first speech, he would, inter alia, have said that

it is the government's aim to involve blacks at as many levels of decision-making as may affect their interests. The further constitutional development of blacks enjoys the government's highest priority, and the government has committed itself to negotiate formulae with black leaders aimed at the realisation of the participation of blacks in political decision-making processes.

In this process conflicting aspirations and claims would have had to be reconciled, and the participants in the negotiating process would have had to be prepared to relinquish predetermined non-negotiable positions so as to find solutions which were mutually acceptable. This involved the search for the general good.

Other issues he would have touched upon included the following:

• The re-instatement of the South African citizenship of blacks, including those who lived in 'independent' homelands and self-governing homelands.
• The accommodation of all blacks' legitimate political aspirations within South Africa, which involved their qualifying for the exercise of their political rights up to the highest level.
• A commitment to democratic solutions best suited to meet the requirements of justice.

- The recognition of the human worth of all South Africans through the eradication of all forms of discrimination.
- The creation of equal opportunities.

In the end PW Botha's ego and narrow-mindedness were responsible for his own Rubicon. The fact of the matter is that Botha reneged on what was decided at the Military Intelligence College meeting because, angry about the fact that the essence of what ought to have been in his speech appeared in the newspapers a week before it was due to be announced, he decided to abandon the speech, thereby unwittingly causing the quickening of history to which Sampie Terreblanche referred.

CHAPTER 10

ADMINISTERING THE DEATH SENTENCE

Throughout my public service career, the death sentence was a compulsory sentence for capital crimes unless a court could find mitigating circumstances. What amounted to mitigating circumstances was not determined by statute, but developed by the courts by way of precedent.

What this meant, in effect, was that a court who found someone guilty of, for example, murder had to impose the death sentence unless it could find mitigating circumstances. Even if a court could find mitigating circumstances it could still, of its own accord, impose the death sentence.

Following a conviction and the imposition of the death sentence by a division of the Supreme Court – it could only be imposed by the Supreme Court – the convicted person could apply for leave to appeal to the Appellate Division of the Supreme Court. All death penalties had to be confirmed by the state president acting in consultation with members of the cabinet.

Following a conviction and the imposition of the death sentence, the presiding judge was required to write a report in which he or she had the opportunity to add considerations to the judgement that might be pertinent to the state president's decision whether or not to commute the death sentence. Also, the advocate who conducted the state's case had to write a report giving his or her views as to whether or not the death sentence should be commuted. It stands to reason that the defence advocate frequently also made recommendations for the death sentence to be commuted.

These documents and the entire record of proceedings before the relevant division of the Supreme Court, as well as the Appeal Court record if the matter went on appeal to the Appellate Division, were then sent to the Department of Justice for consideration by the state law advisers who were required to assess the entire case, prepare a summary thereof, and make a recommendation regarding the commutation or otherwise of the death sentence.

The state president invariably chaired the meeting of cabinet ministers in consultation with whom he had to decide whether or not to commute the death sentence. The ministers served on this committee on a rotation basis, with the exception of the minister of Justice who always served on the committee. Each person involved in this process received a copy of the entire record of the case and the other documents to which I have referred. This was not a popular responsibility, but it was certainly one that was taken very seriously.

Even before I was appointed to the State President's Office as Chief State Law Adviser in 1984, I had some exposure to this procedure when Pik Botha, my minister at the time, had to do his stint in the cabinet committee. The committee did not meet frequently, as a consequence of which, to my way of thinking, it invariably had too many cases to deal with. It was absolutely impossible for ministers to work through all the records, and they were bound to rely on the summaries prepared by the state law advisers. They could, of course, refer to the record in respect of any aspect of the matter if they were so inclined.

When Pik Botha's turn came to serve on the committee, all the records and other documents were sent to me. I had to peruse them, prepare my own summary, and advise the minister as to whether or not I thought there were grounds upon which the execution of the death sentence could be avoided. I remember that Pik was very upbeat when he returned from his first committee meeting, because he had been able to persuade his colleagues to commute the death sentences of quite a number of those whose sentences had to be considered on that particular occasion.

This job became one of my main but more unpleasant responsibilities when I was appointed as Chief State Law Adviser in the Office of the State President. As mentioned before, he chaired the meetings of the cabinet committee which meant that he had to consider each and every case. Again my function was to go through the entire record, and prepare a further summary and make my own recommendation as to whether or not, in the circumstances of a particular case, the death sentence should be commuted or not. These summaries would then go to the secretary-general of the State President's Office, Jannie Roux, who would indicate whether or not he agreed with my recommendation.

I was always very ambivalent about the death sentence. On the one hand, I had to read evidence of the most horrific crimes imaginable, particularly those against women and children. On the other hand, one could not help but think how damaged a person had to be to commit acts like that. I was also acutely aware of the fact that the vast majority of the people of this country were in the grip of what my anthropology lecturer, Prof. Christoff Hanekom, styled a culture of poverty from which very few managed to escape and which had devastating implications for the physical and emotional wellbeing of many who could not escape from that culture.

From the outset I was very uncomfortable with having to make a definite recommendation for the death sentence to be carried out. If I could find anything that might serve as motivation for commutation, I would recommend accordingly. But if I could find nothing at all, I was obliged to make a recommendation that it be carried out.

Roux almost invariably agreed with my recommendations without reading anything more than the summary I had prepared.

Occasionally, not that infrequently, judges would inform the state president that although they could not find any mitigating circumstances, they would not, if they had a choice in the circumstances of a particular matter, have imposed the death sentence. Almost invariably the state president would heed advice of this nature and commute the death sentence. On occasion the advocate who conducted the prosecution would alert the state president to some pertinent fact, and that too would ordinarily lead to the death sentence being commuted. If the state law advisers, in the course of the preparation of their summary of the matter, discovered anything which indicated that commuting the death sentence would be appropriate, they would recommend that this be done, and their advice would invariably be followed.

After a while I told Roux that I was no longer going to

make positive recommendations for the death sentence to be carried out, but that I would scrutinise the records and all other documents to see whether any fact or consideration which could have a bearing on the outcome of a matter had been overlooked, and alert the state president to any such fact or consideration. Roux continued to make recommendations as to the implementation of the death sentence in matters in which he only had the benefit of my summary. I carried out my decision.

The cabinet committee was by no means a rubber stamp. I have already recounted how Pik Botha returned quite pleased with having succeeded in getting the state president to agree to commuting a number of death sentences. I know that my father, also a trained lawyer with a considerable amount of criminal law experience, took his responsibility very seriously indeed.

On one occasion when an ANC member had been given the death sentence for murder, there were various factors which I considered should have resulted in the death sentence being commuted. When my initial recommendation to this effect did not find favour with the cabinet committee, I asked to speak to the President personally and was granted an audience at which I stated my case as best I could.

That evening Roux, a former general in the Prison Services and a doctor of psychology whose doctoral thesis concerned psychopathy, and who frequently related how he had been witness to over fifty executions, gleefully told me on the *stoep* of the Union Buildings that my attempt to persuade the State President to commute the death sentence had been unsuccessful. He pointed to bright yellow lights at the other end of the city and asked me whether I knew where they were. I didn't. He told me that those were the lights of Pretoria Central Prison – the place where the person whose death sentence I had tried to have commuted would be executed the next day.

In one particular matter I picked up that the presiding judge, a very senior judge of the Transvaal Supreme Court, had sat with one assessor and not two, seemingly because another one could not be found on short notice, in circumstances where he ought to have known that he might have to impose the death sentence. In my summary I alerted the State President to this fact and took the view that since the court was not properly constituted the conviction and the sentence amounted to a nullity. The Minister of Justice, Kobie Coetsee, and his advisers did not agree. He proposed, instead, that in the circumstances the death sentence should be commuted.

On this occasion the State President sided with me and stuck to his guns, as a consequence of which Coetsee was obliged to put a stated case before the Appellate Division of the Supreme Court for a decisive ruling as to whether or not the court of first instance had been properly constituted. In the event, the Appellate Division found that it had not been properly constituted, and the accused had to be tried from scratch.

Not unsurprisingly letters for clemency, or even court applications for a stay of execution, would be sent or delivered to the State President's Office at the very last minute. In this regard the policy was not to execute a death penalty in circumstances where there was a pending request for clemency or a pending court application. I had an arrangement with the state president's personal staff immediately to inform one of a number of identified officials at the Department of Justice telephonically the moment any such request or application was received. The responsible officers at the Department of Justice would then see to it that, pending the outcome of the consideration of such request or application, the death penalty would not be executed.

I remember that, on one occasion while the state president's personal staff were still in Cape Town and the rest of the office had already returned to Pretoria following a parliamentary session, a written request for clemency was sent to me in Pretoria by a member of the state president's staff. By then it was a few days old. I immediately phoned one of the responsible officials at the Department of Justice, to learn that the person in question was going to be executed the following morning. In the event I received the request for clemency in the nick of time. To this day I remember the agony I suffered during the brief period of not knowing whether or not that person had been executed without the request for clemency having received proper consideration.

The 'integrity' of the entire system was irreparably damaged when, towards the end of PW Botha's reign, the cabinet committee started reprieving offenders as a result of pressure from the United Nations Organisation. This intervention invariably concerned the plight of ANC members. It is clearly unconscionable to compel courts of law to impose the death sentence without any discretion where no mitigating circumstances are present, only to have an executive body overturn what, in many cases, must have been an excruciatingly difficult exercise of judicial authority, only as a result of political considerations.

Following the commencement of the new constitutional

dispensation in 1994, one of the first tasks of the Constitutional Court was to declare the death sentence unconstitutional by
reason of its inconsistency with the right to life.

CHAPTER 11

MY RESIGNATION AS
CHIEF STATE LAW ADVISER

From 1984 to 1987 I was the Chief State Law Adviser in the State's President's Office. I was relatively young, my post was very senior, and I could provide for my family without difficulty. In short, many would have envied me my position.

However, in January of 1987 I resigned to practise as an advocate at the Cape bar – a move which resulted in me having to build a new career from scratch. In what follows I relate how this came about.

In South Africa the traditional long summer vacation is during the months of December and January. In 1986 South Africa still had beach apartheid. This meant that certain beaches were allocated for the exclusive use of whites, and others for the exclusive use of the Coloureds, blacks, etcetera.

The tricameral constitutional system provided for three houses of parliament; one in which whites were represented, one in which Coloureds were represented, and one in which Indians were represented. The leader of the majority Labour Party in the chamber for Coloured people, and the chairman of the Minister's Council in that chamber, was Reverend Allan Hendrickse. He was also a member of PW Botha's cabinet.

During the 1986 December vacation, Hendrickse and other senior members of the Labour Party decided to stage a public act of protest by swimming at a 'white' beach near Port Elizabeth, the city from which Hendrickse hailed. This act of defiance was widely publicised, and PW Botha was furious. (Ironically, it later turned out that the particular beach was in fact a 'Coloured' beach and not a 'white' beach.) PW Botha probably spent the rest of his own vacation at the Wilderness, near George, fuming and thinking about what he was going to say to Hendrickse at the first cabinet meeting of 1987. At that cabinet meeting he lambasted Hendrickse as only he could, and the latter (unnecessarily) apologised for his act of defiance.

At the time my office was opposite that of Jannie Roux, the secretary-general of the State President's Office, who was previously attached to the Department of Correctional Services. As I have said, he is a psychologist who did his doctorate on psychopathy, who was fond of relating that he had witnessed more than fifty executions, and that he had conducted many interviews with Breyten Breytenbach, the famous South African writer/poet, when the latter was in jail. I have a recollection that Breytenbach subsequently described Roux in less than flattering language.

During the lunch hour on the day of the cabinet meeting when Hendrickse had been taken to task for his dip at the wrong beach, Roux came into my office with a transcript of what had been said at the cabinet meeting regarding Hendrickse's conduct. Naturally this was in Afrikaans. He then asked me, without explaining, to translate the transcript into English.

I set about this task not knowing what the purpose of it was. I was soon to find out. That evening on the SABC's eight o'clock national news broadcast the entire transcript was read by André le Roux, an SABC journalist and friend of mine. I was utterly disgusted. Not only was there, in my view, no need for PW Botha to have been so harsh on Hendrickse, nor for Hendrickse to apologise, but in my book, once a man has tendered an apology, that is the end of the matter. Not so for PW Botha. He wanted the country to know how thoroughly he had taken Hendrickse to task for his insubordination.

The next morning I discussed this development with two gentlemen whom I regarded as my friends. They were Daan Prinsloo, who headed the political section of the State President's Office, and Jack Viviers, PW Botha's press liaison officer. I told them that I was so disgusted by what had happened that I was considering tendering my resignation. They encouraged me to do so. It did not occur to me to ask them why they did not think that it would be appropriate for them to resign as well.

I later established why they were so keen for me to resign. Subsequent to my resignation they told me that PW Botha had decided that I should replace Jannie Roux, a veritable yes-man, as secretary-general of the State President's Office. This would have been in line with his decision to make me responsible for negotiating with Mandela – a matter about which I give an account in an earlier chapter.

Whereas Prinsloo hated the idea of Roux being his boss, he would also not have liked me to be his boss for the simple reason, as Eschel Rhoodie previously had occasion to point out, that Prinsloo himself wanted to be the boss. (Eschel Rhoodie was the head of the Department of Information under Dr Connie Mulder, and responsible for the famous 'Infogate' scandal during which it was revealed that the government was publishing a seemingly privately owned English newspaper, which supported its policies, with state funds.)

The next day I resigned by filling out the appropriate resignation form without first telling PW Botha or Roux. Roux was furious. At a meeting of section heads he took me to task for not telling him in advance, and clearly relished the moment when I had to go and explain myself to PW Botha. He actually waited for me to come out of PW Botha's office at the top of the stairs in Tuynhuys, the presidential office in Cape Town. He must have been very disappointed when I reappeared none the worse for the experience.

I told PW Botha in no uncertain terms why I had elected to resign. His response was that I had clearly become the victim of international humanism. I just smiled. His mind immediately turned to more important things. A general election was soon to be held, and my resignation could be a source of embarrassment to him. I gave my word that I would do nothing to embarrass him. In retrospect, I should not have done so.

Later I went to say goodbye to PW Botha. It was a brief affair. He wished me well and told Captain Ehlers, his private secretary, to give me a clothes brush as a parting gift. He seemed to have had a large supply. I reminded him that when we discussed my resignation, he had expressed concern about the possible negative effect it could have for him during the forthcoming election, and reminded him of my assurance in this regard. (I was approached by the press about my resignation, but simply said that I had been admitted, many years previously in 1978, as an advocate of the High Court, and that I had decided to pursue a career as an advocate. This was true as far as it went.)

In the event I told him that he would have seen that I kept my promise. He seemed annoyed by having been reminded of the fact, and I left without further ado. I have not seen him nor spoken to him since.

CHAPTER 12

DENIS WORRALL

If PW Botha contributed to making 1987 a memorable year for me, Denis Worrall outdid him.

Ironically, I first met Worrall, a professor of political science at Rhodes University and editor of a publication called *New Nation*, when he addressed a public meeting, shortly after joining the National Party, in support of my father's candidature in the run-up to a general election in 1973. He is a charismatic person of obvious intelligence, and a gifted orator.

His capabilities are best illustrated by the fact that he was able to win the traditional United Party parliamentary seat, Gardens, for the National Party a few years later – a feat which even Dawie de Villiers, a popular former Springbok rugby captain and later a cabinet minister and leader of the National Party in the Cape Province, was unable to repeat.

Thereafter, also in 1973, I, in my capacity as chairperson of the student branch of the National Party at Stellenbosch, invited Worrall to address a public National Party meeting at the university. It was a huge success and Worrall was formidable, particularly during question time.

He was subsequently elected to represent the National Party in parliament, and then appointed by PW Botha as the vice-chair, under Alwyn Schlebusch, of the President's Council, a body which, *inter alia*, served as a deadlock-breaking mechanism following the introduction, in 1984, of the tricameral parliamentary system. This was a cynical device by which the National Party could ensure that, in the event of there being a deadlock between the National Assembly (where whites were represented) and any of the houses of Representatives (where Coloureds were represented) and/or Delegates (Indians), the majority in the National Assembly would prevail.

Schlebusch, a good friend of PW Botha, disliked his ambitious vice-chair, and prevailed upon Botha to appoint him as an ambassador. Botha obliged, and Worrall was appointed as ambassador to Australia where, by all accounts, he acquitted himself exceptionally well.

In 1984 the Coventry Four saga played itself out in the United Kingdom. Three employees of Kentron, a subsidiary of Armscor, and one employee of Armscor itself were arrested in Coventry and charged with having conspired to export to South Africa, in contravention of customs and excise legislation, parts capable of application in military equipment. Since I was responsible for securing the release on bail of the Coventry Four and the subsequent variation of the conditions of bail which allowed them to return to South Africa, I frequently visited the United Kingdom during that year. Marais Steyn was South Africa's ambassador at the time, and he gave me free reign.

When I commenced managing the Coventry Four case, I was still law adviser to the Department of Foreign Affairs. However, during that same year I became Chief State Law Adviser in the State President's Office, but was required to continue handling the Coventry Four matter.

Following the South African government's decision not to

allow the Coventry Four to return to England, to stand trial on charges relating to arms smuggling, as an act of reprisal for the fact that six persons who were wanted by the South African police were given shelter in the British consulate in Durban, I had to go back to England to prepare a case in which the defence requested that the warrants for the arrest of the four South Africans be set aside.

By then a couple of developments had taken place. Worrall had replaced Marais Steyn as the South African ambassador to the Court of St James, and Malcolm Rifkind, a Scottish lawyer, had been appointed deputy minister at the Foreign Office. (Previously Steyn and I had dealt directly with the foreign minister, Sir Geoffrey Howe, who was more interested in the fact that the famous South African athlete, Zola Budd, had been given British citizenship in record time, than in the Coventry Four matter. Of Howe, Denis Healey, deputy leader of the Labour Party, had previously said that to be attacked by Sir Geoffrey is like being savaged by a dead sheep.)

Worrall assumed a much more hands-on approach and was also, understandably, very eager to ingratiate himself with the Foreign Office. (Relations between South Africa and the United Kingdom were at an all-time low because of the incident.)

When Worrall and I went to see Rifkind about the matter, Worrall was extremely apologetic and did not attempt to defend the South African government's decision. I was much more aggressive. I told Rifkind that, as a lawyer, he ought to know that what was happening at the consulate in Durban was contrary to the most basic principles of international law, a system of law to which the Law Officers of the Crown had made an enormous contribution. I also told him that I was sure that he had in his possession an opinion by the Law Officers to the effect that the provision of shelter to South African citizens in the Durban British consulate was contrary to international law. He did not respond to this.

I know that, subsequently, Worrall went to see Rifkind on his own. I was much too outspoken. He also put pressure on me to advise the South African government to let the Coventry Four return to England to stand trial there. I declined to do this, but informed Pik Botha of the request. Botha told me to tell Worrall to do his job and defend the South African government's decision, or be recalled.

Not realising that I was no longer attached to the Department of Foreign Affairs, Worrall also acted as if I was under his authority and instructed me to prepare a position paper on the Coventry Four matter for circulation among British members of parliament. I remember that this request was made late on a Friday and that I was tired. To his amazement, I declined to do so.

After he had left the embassy, however, I decided that I would oblige him, and prepared a position paper. I telephoned him at Highveld, the official residence of the South African ambassador in London, to tell him that I would prepare the paper, and asked him how I should get it to him. It was then that I was invited to lunch at Highveld on the Sunday. It was the last thing I wanted to do, but I accepted the invitation and took the position paper to Highveld on the Sunday.

Before lunch, Worrall and I talked in his study and I noticed an original cartoon which had appeared in a South African newspaper depicting my father sending Worrall to the 'colonies'. It suggested that my father was responsible for Worrall having been appointed as ambassador to Australia. My father had a very similar cartoon with the same theme, and I told Worrall about it. I asked him whether he believed that my father was responsible for him having been sent to Australia. I told him that Schlebusch had been responsible for that decision. Subsequent events strongly suggest that he did not believe me.

When the Eminent Persons Group (referred to in the chapter on Nelson Mandela) visited South Africa in 1985, it held negotiations with a South African government delegation led by my father. I was a member of the delegation, and Worrall attended the meeting in an observer capacity. At that meeting he apologised to me for not knowing, at the time when I was in London to handle the Coventry Four case, that I was no longer an official in the Department of Foreign Affairs, but Chief State Law Adviser in the President's Office. He had no authority to tell me to prepare the position paper, not because I was no longer an official in the Department of Foreign Affairs, but because I was a state law adviser who, to the best of my knowledge, cannot be ordered to prepare such documents. He probably assumed that my being the president's Chief State Law Adviser put me in a position in which I could influence PW Botha's decisions in respect of his political career. He obviously did not know me well enough to know that I would never have resorted to such tactics.

The year 1987 was general election year in South Africa. I was with my father when he made a call to Worrall in London to ask him whether he would be prepared to represent the National Party in the election in the Maitland constituency. (It will be recalled that he had previously represented the Gardens constituency as a National Party member of parliament.)

Worrall was non-committal, and said that he would think about the proposition. My father and I suspected that Worrall intended to make himself available as a candidate in my father's constituency, and the offer of the candidature for the Maitland constituency was, at least in part, an attempt to draw him out, and in part an attempt to forestall this.

A few days later Worrall announced his intention to resign as ambassador and to oppose my father as an independent candidate in the May general election. Another eminent person, Wynand Malan, a friend of my father and the member of parliament for Randburg, also announced that he would contest his constituency as an independent candidate in a loose alliance with Worrall. In Stellenbosch, the daughter of a former National Party member of parliament and sister of the well-known athlete, Danie Malan, Dr Esther Lategan, also announced that she would contest the Stellenbosch constituency as an independent candidate, in alliance with Worrall and Malan, against the National Party incumbent, Piet Marais.

Worrall had powerful and significant backing. First and foremost was the Rupert family. Johann Rupert had returned from London to report to his father, Anton Rupert, with whom my father had always been on good terms, that he had exciting news, namely that Worrall would contest the Helderberg constituency. He also had the backing of Margaret Thatcher, as evidenced by the fact that her Conservative Party's chief organiser in Scotland came to South Africa to assist Worrall in his election campaign. I would attribute this to the way in which PW Botha treated her foreign secretary, Sir Geoffrey Howe, the acrimonious exchange of letters between them concerning Mandela's release (both stories are related elsewhere), and the general decline in the relationship between South Africa and the United Kingdom. After all, my father was the most senior cabinet minister and the leader of PW Botha's National Party in the Cape Province.

I knew from the moment Worrall made his announcement that my father had a serious fight on his hands. I was serving my notice month at the President's Office, and remember that secretary-general Jannie Roux said at a meeting of senior executives that Worrall obviously had no prospect of winning the Helderberg constituency. I told him that I did not agree, and pointed out that Kuils River, a predominantly Afrikaans-speaking town with approximately eight thousand Nationalist voters, had been excised from the Helderberg constituency after the previous election.

Other factors worked against my father. For example, a Malawian priest had applied for his children to be admitted to the distinguished Rhenish School for Girls. My father supported the application, but it was turned down by the then minister of Education, FW de Klerk. My father's sense of loyalty was such that he never disclosed that he had made representations to De Klerk to accede to this request.

Also, the government was not making any significant progress with the burning issue of the accommodation of black people's political aspirations, and states of emergency had to be proclaimed to curtail violence in black townships. There was also widespread dismay as a result of PW Botha's hardline image and, in particular, his disastrous Rubicon speech. Worrall skilfully capitalised on this, and presented himself and his fellow independent candidates as people with a vision.

There were many interesting developments in the run-up to the election. For example, Somerset West is the main town in the constituency. A number of its prominent citizens paid for a full-page advertisement in the local newspaper in which they expressed their dismay at Worrall's decision. The thrust of this message was that although they would have welcomed Worrall's contribution to South African politics, they considered it inappropriate of him to have elected to oppose a leading reformist National Party member of parliament.

Worrall conducted an American-style campaign. When he addressed public meetings, he would enter the hall to the soundtrack of *Chariots of Fire* (the song used by Thatcher to the same end) and flashing lights. On relatively still days he would appeal for support from the inhabitants of Somerset West with a loud-hailer from the basket of a hot-air balloon. He had hundreds of volunteers doing house calls on his behalf. His newspaper advertisements were colourful and persuasive. In short, he was staging an election campaign the likes of which had never been seen in South African politics.

In addition, many prominent and well-respected people, some of them former supporters of my father, sided with Worrall. Among them were, for example, Prof. Daniel Louw, a professor of theology at the University of Stellenbosch and long-time family friend, and Prof. Sampie Terreblanche, an erstwhile friend and confidant of my father; also Jan Boland Coetzee, a renowned wine maker and former Springbok rugby player, and Divan Serfontein, a popular Springbok rugby captain.

As time went on, the contest in Helderberg became the focus of public attention not only nationwide, but internationally. My father, being a representative of the National Party, had limited access to funds. He could only rely on his allotted share of the funds which the National Party made available to its many candidates, no matter that he was responsible for the collection of the lion's share thereof. Worrall seemingly had endless resources.

At the time my brother, Van Heerden, was working at *Die Burger*, a Cape Town-based daily newspaper, as a political correspondent. He was an exceptionally good journalist with lots of political sense. He was also a perfectionist with impressive academic qualifications. At the time he had a BA honours degree in philosophy, as well as an honours degree in journalism which he obtained *cum laude* under the discerning tutelage of an ex-editor of *Die Burger* and a hard taskmaster, Prof. Piet Cillié. In later life he also obtained a law degree. Neither of us supported the National Party, but, as previously, would assist our father in his campaign.

At an informal meeting involving, *inter alia*, my father, my brother and me, the National Party organiser responsible for my father's constituency (who also had other constituencies entrusted to his care), and the chairperson of the National Party in the constituency, it was decided to publish a constituency-based newspaper for circulation in the Helderberg constituency in support of my father's campaign. My brother and I were put in charge.

The responsibility was assigned to us at difficult times in our respective lives. As *Die Burger's* political correspondent, it was required of my brother literally to work day and night. He had very little time to contribute to our effort. However, he found time to do so, but at a price. He was almost not present when his second son and namesake was born, and had occasion only for infrequent subsequent visits. Van Heerden junior matured into a brilliant, gifted and compassionate boy. He was a good sportsman, pianist, scholar, actor and, above all, orator – a skill that he inherited from his father, and was honed with his father's assistance. Despite his achievements, he was a generous, kind and self-effacing young man when he tragically died at the age of 17, when his school's microbus, which was transporting a group of students to a plays festival in Bloemfontein, overturned *en route* as a result of a burst rear tyre. He and his brother, Chris, were exceptionally good friends of mine. To this day I cherish, and frequently wear, the sweater depicting the name of the play in which he would have participated at the Bloemfontein festival. His untimely death was the biggest tragedy ever to befall my family.

I, too, was in a predicament of major proportions. I had resigned from the President's Office and had joined the Cape bar. I had to do four months' pupillage and write a bar exam before I could even begin to earn an income as an advocate. I had a wife and three children to support. I could have used my five months' accumulated leave to do my pupillage and then serve out my notice month. That would have provided me with a not insignificant income during the period of my pupillage. For reasons of principle, I elected not to do so.

However, the bar exam had to be taken seriously, and a lot of study was required, particularly for someone who had been specialising in public law for so long and had no first-hand experience of a civil or criminal law practice. Taking on the responsibility of producing a newspaper with the assistance only of my brother, who was himself working under extreme pressure, turned out to be a serious threat to my prospects of passing the bar exam. However, it had to be done.

Although I could type reasonably well, having learned to do so during my university vacations when I worked for a local newspaper in George, I was computer-illiterate. By that time *Die Burger* had a computerised system, and my brother was able to do the layout of pages on-screen. I would go to *Die Burger's* offices and type as many 'stories' as I could into the computer, and transfer them to my brother's access point. Later during the night he would edit what I had written and make up the pages of the newspaper as he progressed.

At the time my father was described by the *Cape Argus* as the best constituency member of parliament in the country, a compliment which was not exaggerated and which he deserved. As a member of the Provincial Council of the Cape, he used to travel to George, his constituency at the time, every weekend to conduct interviews with voters who had problems.

Despite being a minister when he was a member of parliament for the Helderberg constituency, he did the same. He went to Somerset West every weekend, and announced in *Die Burger* the fact that he would be there to be consulted by the voters. Writing after his death in January 2006, Prof. Andreas van Wyk, previously vice chancellor of the University of Stellenbosch, and before that director-general of the Department of Constitutional Development and Planning, of which my father was the minister, wrote in *Die Burger* that every Saturday the voters of Helderberg could visit their member of parliament, the second most powerful man in the land, in his humble little office in Somerset West.

Van Heerden and I had many photographs which depicted the fact that my father (and my mother) were very involved in their constituency, and we capitalised by publishing many of them. We produced attractive, informing and punchy newspapers without any typographical errors, in which we presented my father as a constituency MP and an enlightened Nationalist. To this day I believe that, were it not for those newspapers, my father would have lost the election.

Worrall attempted to counter with a newspaper of his own. It was a feeble attempt by comparison, and was discontinued after the first edition.

Having to produce the newspaper took its toll. Van Heerden almost missed being present when his son was born, and worked himself to a virtual standstill. I had to put in a special effort to pass my bar exam as a consequence of the hours which I spent writing material for the newspaper when I should have been studying. I even took on the task of collecting the newspapers at the printers, and taking them to the National Party office in Somerset West and to local shops where, without exception, the shop owners agreed that they could be given to customers at the cash registers. Such was the degree of appreciation for my father's work in his constituency.

On election day I arrived at Somerset West at about four o'clock in the afternoon. I went to the old Somerset West town hall, the largest polling station and the place where vote counting took place. On my arrival my worst fears were confirmed. I immediately sensed that this was going to be the closest of contests. I also remember that Peter Pullen, my father's press liaison officer, greeted me as I got out of the car with 'We're creaming them.' I knew that he was absolutely wrong. I had been to too many such events not to know instinctively that this was a cliffhanger.

I assisted for a while at the town hall, and then accompanied my mother to her brother's residence where she went to refresh herself. When we returned to the town hall she said to me that I should not be disappointed if the margin of my father's victory was small. I didn't share with her my apprehension that it might not even be a victory.

I should mention that by that time my father had lost his voice completely. In his younger days as an attorney he was also an auctioneer, and overtaxed his vocal cords to such an extent that he had to have an operation when he became older. As a result of this operation his voice was hoarse and could not withstand much strain.

I recall that on our arrival at the town hall we were assured by Jimmy Otto, previously the Helderberg constituency's member of the Provincial Council and a good friend, that my father had won the election and that they were only counting the last votes. Reassured by this information, we went to the front of the town hall where a large crowd had assembled in the early hours of the morning. There were at least as many Worrall supporters as there were Heunis supporters, if not more, and television crews and the press, local and international, were there in numbers.

We waited for a long time, but to no avail. The election officer did not make an appearance. I realised that a re-count was in the offing. After many hours of waiting, my brothers and I went to the National Party office in the town hall, where we were told that my father had won by a very small margin.

When, finally, the result was announced, my father had won

the election by 39 votes, and the candidates appeared before the assembled crowd. The vociferous National Party supporters prevented Worrall from speaking. The Worrall supporters did the same to my father. They had no way of knowing that it was not necessary because he could not speak at all.

However, my father's dismay at the outcome, for which he should have been grateful, was evident in the television broadcasts of the event. Instead of being exuberant, he was dejected. Properly handled, his victory should have been depicted as a major one – because that is what it was. He had won against all the odds.

In Randburg, Wynand Malan thoroughly thrashed Glenn Babb, his competent National Party opponent and a former diplomat. In Stellenbosch, unknown Esther Lategan made a telling inroad into Piet Marais's previous majority.

None of these facts was acknowledged, particularly not within the National Party. My father's political career was dealt a severe blow.

When he announced his resignation as a member of parliament (and also as a member of the cabinet) during May 1989, many people commented. The comment that hurt him most was that of Wynand Malan, an erstwhile friend, who said that he had resigned because he didn't have the stomach to face Worrall in another election. Worrall, on the other hand, praised my father as having been a true reformist and the driving force behind the enlightened National Party initiatives which preceded his political demise.

In February 2006 Worrall paid tribute to my father by attending his funeral – something which I greatly appreciated, and had occasion to convey to him publicly.

CHAPTER 13

MY FATHER'S CAREER AND RESIGNATION IN BRIEF OUTLINE

The pre-1994 constitutional dispensation in South Africa was characterised, *inter alia*, by geographic constituencies represented in parliament as well as in the various provincial councils.

Following the completion of his articles at the prestigious Cape Town law firm, Silberbauers, where he was offered a partnership, my father returned to his home town, George, where he established his own law firm in which he was assisted by his brother, Jim. He was a very active member of civil society, and my mother used to say that if all the societies to which he belonged held monthly meetings on different days, he would not be able to attend them all. He was, *inter alia*, a founder member of the Round Table, the president of the Agricultural Society, and very active in the affairs of the George South Dutch Reformed Church. He was also an exceptionally good court lawyer, and as such won the respect of all George's communities, notably the Coloured community, the members of which frequently referred to him as 'oom [uncle] Chris' because he represented them to good effect in many court cases. If they could not pay, they could not pay.

Since my father was also the chairman of the local branch of the National Party, he came into frequent contact with PW Botha, George's member of parliament. Having previously been the head organiser of the National Party in the Cape, a position to which he was appointed by Prime Minister DF Malan, Botha was an 'imported' member of parliament since he came from the Free State and was not a son of George. As a consequence my father was frequently asked to oppose Botha as MP for George and, given his popularity in the town, I have no doubt that he would have been able to oust him if he wanted to. However, since my father was very firm in his view that he would never oppose a sitting member of parliament, he never acceded to these requests. He was only 29 years old when he was elected George's member of the Cape Provincial Council, and in 1965, when I was in standard six, he was elected as a member of the executive council of that Provincial Council, the equivalent of a provincial minister.

In his capacity as MPC for George, he naturally had to work in close relationship with the member of parliament, but PW Botha was never part of my father's circle of intimate friends.

My father's public speeches were characterised by two things, namely the need for respect for one's fellow human beings, and the need for change to accommodate the legitimate political aspirations of the majority of South Africans who were denied participation in the country's constitutional dispensation.

I was very young when I listened to a speech which he made at nearby Blanco on 16 December, the Day of the Covenant, the date on which Afrikaners commemorated the victory of the Voortrekkers over Dingaan's impis at Blood River – four hundred brave 'boers' with guns and cannons fighting 8 000 equally brave Zulus armed with spears.

My father exhorted his audience not to view the day as one

on which the victory of one population group over another was celebrated, but rather as one which should inspire South Africa's diverse population groups to overcome their differences and find a *modus vivendi* in a South Africa that belonged to all.

He was a particularly good constituency representative, and as I have said travelled to George from Cape Town each weekend to be able to consult with his constituents. This sense of responsibility stood him in good stead when, in later years, he was opposed by Denis Worrall in the parliamentary election for the Helderberg constituency of which he was then the member of parliament.

In 1970, the year during which I did my military service, my father was elected as member of parliament for the False Bay constituency. Following the re-demarcation of constituencies, he subsequently became the member of parliament for the Helderberg constituency of which Somerset West and Kuils River were the main towns.

In 1972 he was appointed Deputy Minister of Economic Affairs, in 1974 Minister of Indian Affairs, and in 1976 Minister of Economic Affairs. Subsequently he served variously as Minister of Home Affairs, Minister of Transport, and Minister of Constitutional Development and Planning. He served first in John Vorster's cabinet, and subsequently in PW Botha's cabinet.

In an article by Andreas van Wyk, styled 'Chris Heunis: underestimated leader', which appeared in *Die Burger* of 4 February 2006, shortly after my father's death, Van Wyk, who had been director-general of the Department of Constitutional Development and Planning, and subsequently vice chancellor and rector of the University of Stellenbosch, referred to PW Botha as my father's political mentor. Nothing could be further from the truth. My father was probably too loyal a member of the National Party, and probably overestimated his capacity to change the National Party from within as a prelude to necessary political changes, but PW Botha was never his mentor. Van Wyk himself described my father as the most enlightened and one of the most intelligent members of PW Botha's cabinet, who was intellectually and emotionally much more convinced of the need for change than the theatrical Pik Botha, the doubting Kobie Coetsee and the previously reserved FW de Klerk. PW Botha could simply not have been the mentor of someone like my father. I know he was nothing of the kind.

Closer to the truth is Van Wyk's remark that as long as my father enjoyed PW Botha's unreserved support, he could live out his enlightened instincts as Minister of Constitutional Development and Planning. Van Wyk rightly pointed out that my father was a lawyer and instinctive anti-militarist who viewed the rise of the so-called securocrats under Botha with concern. He was uncomfortable in the State Security Council, and when his department attempted to make contact with the ANC, he tried to protect his senior officials against the mighty security establishment – although not always successfully. This is a reference to the fact that the security clearance of Fanie Cloete and Kobus Jordaan, two senior officials in my father's department, had been withdrawn following talks with members of the ANC.

Van Wyk also recounts how Constitutional Development's proposal to PW Botha for a ground-breaking opening speech at the Natal National Party congress during 1985 succumbed before the joint influence of Botha's own office, the securocrats and the Transvaal conservatives. The subsequent Rubicon crisis, caused by excessive marketing by Pik Botha and his diplomats, hailed the end of PW Botha's reform willingness.

I have little doubt that Botha's 'own office' did not attempt to divert him from what he was supposed to announce in the first place. Clearly, if called upon, Prinsloo would have had no choice but to assist Botha with the preparation of the speech he ultimately delivered.

I deal elsewhere with the true facts of the infamous Rubicon speech. Van Wyk's assessment is, however, right inasmuch as, notwithstanding the fact that my father was allowed to lay the groundwork, principally through the abolition of many apartheid laws, for a democratic constitutional dispensation, Botha was never going to allow blacks to participate fully in any future South African political dispensation. When this became clear their relationship came to an end and precipitated my father's resignation from the cabinet and from parliament.

My father's political career almost ended in 1976 within a few days after he had been appointed by John Vorster as Minister of Economic Affairs. On the Saturday following his appointment he had to attend a meeting of the Cape provincial National Party caucus of members of parliament in Cape Town under the chairmanship of PW Botha, then the provincial leader of the Cape National Party. Botha had been the author of a policy that the Western Cape was to be an area in which Coloured labour was to be employed in preference to black labour.

At the caucus meeting my father was asked how many black

people were employed by parastatals in the Western Cape. In those years the Department of Economic Affairs was responsible for most large parastatals. Having been appointed to the position of Minister of Economic Affairs only a few days earlier, my father did not know the answer and responded by saying that he considered it unfair to be expected to answer such a question so soon after his appointment. PW Botha, however, instructed him to answer the question, whereupon my father told him to go to hell, took his briefcase and left the meeting. He was on the verge of resigning, but following intervention by many people, including Dr Piet Cillié, the editor of *Die Burger* at the time, he relented and decided to stay on in John Vorster's cabinet.

My father's greatest contribution to making South Africa a better place to live in had nothing to do with what he was able to achieve within the narrow constraints of National Party policy. It had everything to do with the personal relationships he had established with people, regardless of their race, creed or colour.

It was never National Party policy that the political aspirations of the Coloured and Indian communities should be realised in a geo-political entity such as a self-governing or independent homeland. There were people who adhered to the view that this should have been National Party policy, foremost amongst whom was Dr Andries Treurnicht, leader of the Transvaal National Party and a member of John Vorster's cabinet as well as PW Botha's first cabinet. I remember once asking Piet Vorster, John Vorster's son who was a contemporary of mine at Stellenbosch University, why his father tolerated Treurnicht, to which Piet responded that his father believed that if Treurnicht was given enough rope he would hang himself. Those were prophetic words, because that is exactly what happened, albeit not during Vorster's tenure as prime minister but during that of his successor, Botha.

The National Party was therefore faced with the challenge of accommodating the political aspirations of these communities within the Republic of South Africa as such. The Department of Constitutional Development and Planning, of which my father was the minister at the time, was charged with the responsibility of developing constitutional proposals to this end. It proposed a tricameral parliamentary system in which white people would be represented in one chamber, the Coloureds in another chamber, and the Indians in yet another.

In respect of so-called 'general affairs', i.e. matters of concern to the community at large, the three chambers would act as one parliament with legislation having to be passed by all three. In respect of so-called 'own affairs', i.e. matters concerning a particular community only, they would be autonomous legislatures in their own right, and would function independently of one another.

As already explained, the fact that, in respect of general affairs, they functioned as chambers of one parliament and could only adopt legislation if consensus could be reached, brought with it the possibility of deadlocks. For this reason the constitutional proposals also envisaged the establishment of a President's Council which would function as a deadlock-breaking mechanism, apart from its other functions. The way in which the President's Council was constituted would ensure a built-in majority for the majority party in the House of Assembly – the white chamber – and therefore, in the event of a deadlock, the governing party in the House of Assembly would virtually be assured of a favourable decision by the President's Council were a matter to be referred to it for purposes of deadlock-breaking.

The proposals also envisaged an executive, as opposed to a titular, state president who would have the power of deciding whether or not to refer a deadlock to the President's Council for determination. He would not, however, be obliged to refer any such deadlock to the President's Council.

Once the cabinet had decided to approve these constitutional proposals, my father had to sell them to the various provincial congresses of the National Party and, ultimately, to its federal congress. This was successfully accomplished. However, if the new dispensation was to have any credibility whatsoever it was critically important that Reverend Allan Hendrickse's Labour Party should participate in the new dispensation. The Labour Party had a measure of credibility. Having won elections for Coloured persons in the Coloured Representative Council, a legislative body with limited legislative capacity in respect of Coloured people, the party rendered it unworkable by boycotting it. After protracted negotiations my father managed to persuade the leadership of the Labour Party, notably Hendrickse and Currie, to participate in the tricameral system. This was a major *coup* at the time.

The cabinet had decided that whether or not the tricameral system would be implemented was something about which the white electorate would have the final say by means of a referendum. In the event the outcome of the referendum was favourable for the implementation of the tricameral system, and it was implemented in terms of the 1983 constitution which commenced in 1984.

Before its commencement, and over time, the tricameral system was severely criticised. For example, in *The Other Side of History* Van Zyl Slabbert refers to it as 'pathetic' and as a type of 'constitutional fraud'.

Particularly during the 1980s my father was a champion for constitutional reform within the National Party. In his autobiography FW de Klerk states that he was one of the giants of the reform movement and should receive full credit for the great contribution that he made during the PW Botha period.

In an article styled 'Heunis a loyal MP, but with vision', which was published after his death, in *The Herald* on 30 January 2006, he was described by Patrick Cull as 'deeply frustrated with his inability to drive the party forward to what he knew and accepted was the inevitable political solution'. He was also referred to as a consummate politician revelling in the Westminster-style cut-and-thrust debate, who remarked privately when Progressive Federal Party leader Frederik van Zyl Slabbert announced his resignation at the end of the no-confidence debate in 1986 that there was 'nobody left in the House to debate with'. The same article describes the tricameral constitution as a

> tortuous document with its concepts of 'own affairs' and 'general affairs', and this much he [my father] acknowledged when he told a public meeting ahead of a referendum on bringing Coloureds and Indians into parliament at Port Elizabeth's Feathermarket Hall: 'Even if you don't understand the constitution, vote Yes.'

As recounted in the chapter on the Police's secret fund, PW Botha did not have any sense of the fragility of the tricameral system or, if he had, he could not care less. Following a report by the President's Council on the Group Areas Act, he laid down guidelines for new legislation which would have lacked some aspects of the Act, whilst tightening others. It was destined to be unacceptable to the Coloured and Indian houses of parliament. My father, being the responsible minister, had no enthusiasm for the proposed legislation, and he thought that it would cause relations with the Labour Party to deteriorate and could even have threatened the continued existence of the tricameral parliament. As FW de Klerk recounts in *The Last Trek – A New Beginning*, he was right. The Coloured and Indian chambers refused to participate in any way, and instead launched a boycott which threatened to bring parliament to a standstill.

My father, De Klerk and (at the time) deputy minister Roelf Meyer held discussions with Allan Hendrickse over a period of two days, and between them they ultimately achieved a compromise. The text of a joint statement which would be issued jointly by Hendrickse and my father was agreed, but Botha's approval first had to be obtained. De Klerk recounts how he was with my father when he spoke with Botha by telephone. He listened while the essence of the agreement was explained to Botha, and Botha gave his approval for it. He was not happy, but said that they could go ahead with their announcement. They did so, and the crisis was defused.

However, at the following cabinet meeting Botha took my father to task for not having properly informed him of the agreement with Hendrickse. My father refuted the charges, and said that he had nothing for which to apologise. De Klerk then told Botha that my father's version was correct, that he had stood beside him when he had received Botha's approval, and that it was unfair to accuse my father of not having obtained proper clearance. Botha stormed out of the meeting in anger, and after some time De Klerk and my father went to speak with him in his office. Without backing down they assured him that they were not trying to challenge his authority, and convinced him to return to the cabinet meeting.

In *Stem uit die Wilderness*, Daan Prinsloo also relates that this was one of the stormiest cabinet meetings ever, and that the irony was that my father was in favour of scrapping the Group Areas Act, but had to steer the new law through parliament notwithstanding the fact that he had frequently warned against the consequences thereof.

Following his explanation of what the legislation would involve, Prinsloo continues by saying that my father conveyed the news of a settlement with the Coloured and Indian leaders telephonically to Botha. It soon became known that Botha was upset by the settlement as well as by the unrelated fact of a caucus meeting which had been convened by De Klerk, ostensibly without his knowledge. Accordingly he used the occasion of the subsequent cabinet meeting to express his dissatisfaction with these and other nuisances ('*lastighede*')! Botha also objected to the way in which my father informed him of the agreement in respect of the contentious law. He criticised the way in which my father's department had handled legislation, and held my father personally responsible. De Klerk argued that if the department had not done what it did, the parliamentary system could have collapsed.

Three generations: Chris Heunis (*left*), Chris junior and Jan Heunis.
Photo: Private collection, Heunis Family

Jan Heunis – a student leader at the University of Stellenbosch in the 70s.
Photo: Edrich, Stellenbosch

The Student Council of the University of Stellenbosch, 1973-1974.
Back row from left: Johan Gelderblom, Cassie Wait, Bertie du Plessis, Hennie van der Merwe, Jan Heunis, Blikkies van Schalkwyk, Pieter Vorster, Leon Kuschke.
Front row from left: Bobby Loubser (Secretary), Retha Rossouw, Prof Jannie de Villiers (Rector and Vice Chancellor), Willem Doman (Chairperson), Adv John Vorster (Chancellor), Pieter Hurter, Jan Hofmeyr (Treasurer). *Photo: Edrich, Stellenbosch*

The NP Student Branch Council, Stellenbosch (1973-1974).
Back row from left: Gawie Nienaber, Johan Loubser, JP Landman, Willie Hayward, Abrie de Swardt, Frans le Roux.
Front row from left: Lita Badenhorst, Andrew Theunissen, Retha Rossouw (Secretary), Jan Heunis (Chairperson), Rassie Malherbe (Vice-chairperson), Yzelle Geldenhuys, Carl Havemann (Treasurer). *Photo: Edrich, Stellenbosch*

Opposite: Current and future National Party leaders of the time. The student NP branch at Stellenbosch – the largest in the country – had regular contact with cabinet ministers. At a meeting in 1972 Minister SP (Fanie) Botha (*second from right*) and Deputy Minister Chris Heunis (*second from left*) paid tribute to the successes of the student branch. *Far right* is Jan Heunis, chairperson of the student branch, and *far left* is his deputy, Johan Gelderblom. *Photo: ProNat*

An agreement on security, based on principles similar to those of the Nkomati Accord, was reached between South Africa and Swaziland in February 1982. It was made public a year later on 31 March 1983. This photograph was taken at the announcement of the accord in Pretoria.
From left: Louis Nel (Deputy Minister of Foreign Affairs), Pik Botha (Minister of Foreign Affairs), RV Dlamini (Swaziland's Minister of Foreign Affairs) and MS Matsebula (Swaziland's Minister of Labour and Public Service).
Photo: Department of Information and Communication

Prime Minister PW Botha and President Samora Machel signing the Nkomati Peace Accord between South Africa and Mozambique, March 1984.
Photo: National Achives of South Africa (NASA), SAB 17390

Prime Minister PW Botha (*middle right*) and President Samora Machel (*middle left*) meeting in the White Coach on the occasion of the signing of the Nkomati Peace Accord, March 1984. *Photo: NASA, SAB 19872*

President Samora Machel and Mr PW Botha during the proceedings surrounding the signing of the Nkomati Peace Accord.
Photo: NASA (SAB 16439)

Members of the special cabinet committee for black constitutional affairs, April 1984.
Back from left: J Weilbach, Dr J Roux, JM van Rooyen, PJVE Pretorius, JHT Mills,
TNH Janson, JA Jordaan, FW de Klerk, BJ du Plessis, L le Grange, TK Mopeli,
L Nel, Dr G van N Viljoen.
Front from left: HJ Coetsee, SS Skosana, Dr PGJ Koornhof, Dr CN Phatudi, JC Heunis,
Dr HWE Ntsanwisi, RF Botha. *Photo: NASA (SAB 18883)*

Prime Minister PW Botha meets the Prime Minister of England, Mrs Margaret
Thatcher, at her country home Chequers, June 1984. F*rom left:* Sir Geoffrey Howe
(British Foreign Secretary), PW Botha, Mrs Margaret Thatcher and Pik Botha (South
African Minister of Foreign Affairs). *Photo: NASA (NAR 371)*

The South African Cabinet, December 1986.

Back row from left: Dr WA van Niekerk (Minister of National Health and Population Development), Rev HJ Hendrickse (Minister without portfolio and Chairman of the Ministers' Council in the House of Representatives), JCG Botha (Minister of Home Affairs and Communication), JWE Wiley (Minister of Environmental and Water Affairs), E van de M Louw (Minister of Transport), A Rajbansi (Minister without portfolio and Chairperson of the Ministers' Council in the House of Delegates), AJ Vlok (Minister of Law and Order).

Middle row from left: DW Steyn (Minister of Economic Affairs and Technology), HJ Coetsee (Minister of Justice), General M de M Malan (Minister of Defence), Dr G van N Viljoen (Minister of Education and Development Aid), PTC du Plessis (Minister of Mineral and Energy Affairs), G Wentzel (Minister of Agricuture), BJ du Plessis (Minister of Finance).

Front row from left: RF Botha (Minister of Foreign Affairs), AL Schlebusch (Minister in the Office of the State President), PW Botha (State President) JC Heunis (Minister of Constitutional Development and Planning), FW de Klerk (Minister of National Education).

Photo: NASA (SAB 19053)

JC (Chris) Heunis, South African Minister of Constitutional Development and Planning, 1985.
Photo: NASA (SAB 17274)

Below: Representatives at the multi-party meeting of Codesa ll (Convention for a Democratic South Africa) at the World Trade Centre near Johannesburg, 1992.
Photo: NASA (SAB 19693)

The astonishing feature of Prinsloo's treatment of this material is that the reader is left in the dark as to exactly what it was that my father and his department were supposed to have done, or failed to do, that caused Botha to become so angry that he actually threatened to dismiss ministers, presumably my father and De Klerk, the provincial leaders of the National Party in the Cape and Transvaal respectively! At least Prinsloo confirms that neither De Klerk nor my father apologised to Botha.

My father was the Minister of Constitutional Development and Planning during the first half of the 1980s. Fanie Cloete was one of his senior advisers during this time. He is now a professor at the University of Stellenbosch. Ich Rautenbach and Rassie Malherbe, other senior advisers, are now professors of law at the University of Johannesburg (formerly the Rand Afrikaans University). The director-general, Andreas van Wyk, became the vice chancellor and rector of the University of Stellenbosch. Willie Breytenbach, another senior official, is also a professor at Stellenbosch University.

Writing in *Die Burger* of 16 February 2006 in an article styled 'Chris Heunis and the erosion of apartheid', Fanie Cloete gives the following exposition of what transpired during that period.

According to him, the cabinet of that time was divided over the maintenance of the apartheid system. The era was characterised by ideological differences between the reformist-minded members of the National Party (my father and Pik Botha, with the support of Stoffel van der Merwe, Barend du Plessis and later also Roelf Meyer and Leon Wessels) and what he refers to as '*bittereinders*' (die-hards) such as FW de Klerk, Magnus Malan and Louis le Grange.

PW Botha's willingness to reform was simply the consequence of the assurances of my father, Pik Botha and others that the National Party could maintain control over the transition process and that it would be able to establish so-called consensus government (involving blacks) within which the National Party would retain a minority veto.

The reformists' personal view frequently differed from their forced public positions. They deliberately wanted to achieve the acceleration of the erosion of apartheid through a Machiavellian strategy to create a more favourable climate for evolutionary constitutional transition to a more democratic dispensation. From 1985 they were frequently confronted, in cabinet committee context and in other conversations, by the intense emotional resistance of the die-hards, who were not convinced of the National Party's capacity to control the outcome of the intended changes. De Klerk's core argument was that any watering down of National Party policy would be tantamount to an in-principle deviation from the policy, and would therefore be the thin end of the wedge.

The security and intelligence services had begun to realise that the end of the armed conflict was in sight. They later attempted to convince the ANC to denounce violence with a view to trumping it at the negotiating table and forcing a consensus-seeking model upon it. This did not work.

Key reforms which systematically eroded apartheid, such as multiracial regional services councils, the watering down of group areas and the preparation by my father and his advisers for negotiations with the UDF, Azapo and other ANC-minded internal groups, finally caused the internal power play between the reformists and the die-hards to come to open confrontation.

The fear of political demise gave the conservative die-hards, backed by the security forces, the upper hand, and resulted in PW Botha turning against my father, who in 1987 was deliberately excluded from any negotiations with Nelson Mandela.

Whether Cloete's scenario is entirely accurate is not the point. The fact remains that when the chips were down and it became clear that something had to be done about black political aspirations, PW Botha in fact turned against my father. I know because he was never in favour of sharing power with black South Africans.

It is entirely true that, particularly during 1985, the year in which PW Botha delivered his disastrous Rubicon speech, my father canvassed tirelessly for meaningful reform initiatives in respect of black political advancement.

In a speech to the Institute of Bankers in Sandton on 13 March 1985, he canvassed the advancement and accommodation of the interests of black communities in all spheres of human endeavour, and spoke of a dedicated determination to achieve a fair solution of all outstanding matters involving the position of blacks, particularly urban blacks. He concluded by confirming that the accommodation of blacks would be an integral part of the ideal 'to shape a better future for all of us'.

In his notes for a speech during the second reading debate of the budget in the National Assembly on 11 April 1985, he referred to the process of reform with a view to long-term goals to improve the quality of life of all South Africans in all spheres of life. He said the following:

> Only an honest conviction to achieve a fairer dispensation for everyone will ensure a successful process of reform.

In his notes for a speech on 9 May 1985, he described his own conviction that all South Africans have a common destiny. One community cannot separate itself from the others, and no one community can plan and execute its future independently of the others.

In a speech to the Afrikaans Cultural Council at Stellenbosch on 29 May 1985, he referred to the importance of the fact that the Afrikaner shares a continent with other peoples and population groups who have precisely the same ideals in respect of freedom as the Afrikaner himself.

The Afrikaner dare not plan to deal with his own ideals of freedom and those of others by subjugating others through the physical and political power which Afrikaners had obtained. Instead, they had to assist others to realise their ideals, and the vicious circle of freedom at the expense of the freedom of others had to be broken. It was necessary to accept that the various population groups had a common interest which would have to be dealt with by common institutions of government, and which would call for co-responsibility for decisions.

At a National Party Information Conference at Barberton on 1 June 1985, he pleaded for recognition of the aspirations of others. He asked that recognition be given to the fact that conflict situations developed because blacks did not have access to effective political mechanisms through which to articulate their aspirations and ideals. He described his political vision as 'white certainty and black hope'.

In a speech before the Natal Chamber of Industries on 20 June 1985, he said:

It is accepted without reservation by the government that re-

form and adjustment are necessary in regard to all our communities, including the black communities.

In that speech he recognised that the urban blacks could not
come into their own through autonomous and self-governing homelands.

All communities must, however, be brought into the political process.

The speech envisaged a process of negotiations involving all
blacks, and referred to the work of the Special Cabinet Committee. There is a note on the speech that, in this regard, he was
experiencing resistance.

In a memorandum containing guidelines for further constitutional development dated 30 September 1985, probably intended for discussion purposes either in the cabinet or in the
Special Cabinet Committee, he noted *inter alia* the following:

- The possibility of black urban communities being accepted as political entities for constitutional purposes.
- The prospect of majority government and protection of
  minority rights through individual rights expressed in a
  bill of rights, coupled with judicial control to be provided
  for in a constitution.
- The possibility of majority government. Planning would
  be necessary for an orderly transitional phase and the protection of constitutional guarantees for the benefit of minority groups, which could not, by definition, presuppose
  equal group participation in the political system. (Imme-

diately prior to the commencement of the multi-party negotiations at Kempton Park in 1993, the government was
still opposed to majority rule.)

- The necessity for new structures of government at the central level of government to replace the existing structures.
- Black political representation in one state up to the highest level possible.
- The establishment of a constitutional court with a control
function in respect of the constitution.

The memorandum contains the following:

> We are committed to the principle of a united, undivided South
> Africa, one citizenship, and universal franchise within structures
> chosen by South Africans. The overriding common denomi-
> nator is our mutual interest in each other's freedom and well-
> being. Our peace and prosperity are indivisible. We accept an
> undivided RSA where all regions and communities within its
> boundaries form part of the South African state, with the right
> to participate in institutions to be negotiated collectively. We
> resolve to pursue peaceful and democratic solutions that sat-
> isfy the requirements of fairness and justice. We believe that a
> democratic system of government, which must accommodate
> all legitimate political aspiration of all the South African com-
> munities, must be negotiated.

In an undated memorandum with the heading 'Key points for
1985', he noted *inter alia* the following:

- The government was striving towards a democratic consti-

tutional system.
- The entitlement of all groups to South African citizenship should be recognised.
- The ideal that there may not be black South African citizens had to be abandoned.
- The principle of a single constitutional framework providing for power-sharing between all groups had to be accepted.
- All groups should have co-responsibility in respect of matters of common interest.
- The principle of universal franchise had to be accepted.
- This had to be achieved through a process of negotiation.
- The agenda should be open, but the government had to have its own plan.

It is incredibly sad that he was not allowed to act upon these insights in 1985. The subsequent years saw states of emergency, an intensification in South Africa's isolation, and untold human suffering.

The Group Areas Act, which provided for separate residential areas for whites, Coloureds and Indians, was still on the statute book. My father was charged with the implementation of this Act. During May 1989 he made an appointment with PW Botha to tell him that he could not negotiate with blacks while he was responsible for that law and others that called for separation between the races.

My father told PW Botha that the discussion of his portfolio was imminent in the National Assembly and that he intended to announce that he would no longer be responsible for the administration of these laws. He also told him that he would prepare a state president's minute in terms of which the application of those laws would be assigned to another minister. He suggested that the appropriate person would the minister of Land Affairs. Botha agreed. My father had the minute prepared and delivered to Botha's private secretary, Captain Ters Ehlers, with a note that his portfolio was destined to be discussed on a specific date and that it was imperative for the State President to sign the minute by, at the latest, the morning of the day on which my father made the announcement in the National Assembly.

On 11 May 1989, having made the announcement in the National Assembly, my father returned to his office where he had a meeting with senior officials of his department. During the meeting he had to take a call from Botha. He was livid about the announcement my father had made. Officials who were at that meeting subsequently told me that they could hear Botha shouting over the phone.

My father told him that he had done nothing Botha had not authorised, but that Botha would hear from him shortly. He put the phone down, adjourned the meeting, sat down and wrote his letter of resignation. His secretary delivered to the State President's Office my father's hand-written resignation.

I was to learn of this shortly before six o'clock on the morning of my first appearance before the South African Appellate Division in Bloemfontein.

It was headline news. Significantly even my father's most liberal opponents, including Denis Worrall, considered it a setback for the progress of the enlightened movement in South Africa. It was, however, sad to read in the *Volksblad*, the newspaper that circulates in the Orange Free State province (as it was at the time) that Wynand Malan, the independent member of parliament for Randburg and long-time friend of my father, had said that my father resigned because he was too scared to face another encounter with Worrall.

This is probably an appropriate point at which to remark that my brother, Van Heerden, and I had become convinced that my father should resign. We both sensed, as confirmed by Fanie Cloete, that he was fighting a losing battle in the National Party, and could not see him realising the democratic ideal in a government headed by PW Botha.

Not once during his subsequent retirement did my father publicly say anything about politics. He involved himself in social work, particularly the care of the elderly in Somerset West. Following his death on 27 January 2006 Gloria Woodland, chairperson of the Helderberg Society for the Aged, *inter alia* wrote in a local newspaper, the *District Mail*:

> Mr Heunis, as the MP for Helderberg and Minister of Economic Affairs, was instrumental in the growth of the Society by enabling us to expand to serve *all* the aged in the community [my emphasis].
>
> His interest in the Society was constant. After he left politics and retired to Somerset West, he was an active volunteer.
>
> He was persuaded to join the Management Board in 1997 and, after a spell as vice-chairman, he took the chair in 2001.

Andreas Van Wyk concludes the article referred to earlier as follows:

And when he left politics, he stayed out, practising as an attorney with his sons in Somerset West. He did not attempt to play along from the sideline.

He died in the intensive care unit of the Vergelegen Medi-Clinic on 27 January 2006.

This is what I said at his memorial service:

'It could be expected of me to say:

- I am my father's eldest son.
- I bear his names.
- My son bears his names.
- I owe him, and his legacy, a duty of honour. I have often failed him. I do not intend to do so now.
- It could be expected of me to say: Since the public record of my father's political legacy is incomplete, also twisted and inaccurate, this duty would have involved setting the record straight, no matter what, as long as it is not done vindictively or in a spirit of retaliation, because if that were the motive, I would be disloyal to his legacy.
- The record of his legacy is incomplete, partly because of the rules by which he lived, one of which dictates that when one leaves public life, it is inappropriate to comment publicly from the sidelines.

'I would now add to this, the following:

- As a consequence of his uncompromising adherence to this

rule, he never publicly set the record straight, no matter how painful the injury, how offensive the lie.

- His record is also incomplete as a result of his sense of loyalty which precluded him from speaking out, even when not doing so caused him grievous harm.

- It is incomplete because uncaring, careless and vindictive people published untruths, or allowed them to go unchallenged, which he refrained from repudiating, precisely because of his adherence to the rules to which I have just referred.

- My father was a tireless champion for reform and, in a sense, it was sad that a man who devoted his life to the pursuit of the democratic ideal, in the fullest sense of the word, was not there when the final steps of the transition process to a fully democratic South Africa were taken. I could have explained why that was so and fully intended doing so, but I have decided not to do so.

- For a while I was consumed by a sense that that was my duty and that that was what I should do, until I read the last speech which he delivered in parliament on 22 May 1989. Through that speech he spoke to me, in the immortal words of Karen Blixen, the author of *Out of Africa*. When floods broke the dam on her farm and the farmworkers tried to repair it, she stopped them and said: 'Let the waters go home to Mombasa.'

- He told me, through that speech, not to attempt to do on his behalf, at least not on this occasion, what he himself had elected not to do.

- I would use his own words, taken from his last speech in the National Assembly, to pay tribute to him.

- He commenced that speech by quoting Omar Khayyam's definition of life:

  'Tis but a Chequer-board of Nights and Days
  Where Destiny with Men for Pieces plays:
  Hither and thither moves, and knights, and slays,
  And one by one back in the Closet lays.

- He acknowledged the insignificance of man and the transience of his existence.
- And then followed: 'Since this is the last piece of legislation I will introduce into this House, honourable members will understand that I stand here with mixed feelings. It is only human for those living and those leading at one particular point in time to think that their own time is one of great moment, of great danger and of great challenge.'
- He was obviously sad. Who would not have been if he had dedicated his life to an ideal and could not be present at the fulfilment thereof?
- But there is also acceptance as there can only be with a person who is at peace with himself. He must therefore have been satisfied with the fact of his resignation and his reasons for it. And then followed the insistence that one should be modest and not value one's own role too highly, and not claim a too-important place in history for oneself, when he said: 'It is right and it is good that this should be so, for this is how men and women become responsible and become involved in the affairs of the community and in the affairs of their country. But for the sake of humility, we who are involved in politics should now and then

pause to look back at the political history of our country, and indeed of mankind … What is clear is that the story of the political history of mankind is a story of continuous growth and change. What is indeed significant is not that change was and is inevitable, but that growth more often than not continued in spite of, rather than because of, the intervention of history's remembered political leaders. It is probably more true to say that history makes men, than that men make history.'

- He said: 'Look, life goes on without you. Don't overestimate your role. The greatest setbacks in the political growth of mankind occurred when able, clever, persuasive politicians interrupted the steady process of change by destructive fervour or, on the other extreme, obstructive obstinacy. Less often found in history books are the names of the vast majority of reasonable people whose day-by-day concerned involvement helped to turn change into growth. Politically it is infinitely more spectacular to be destructive or obstructive than to be builders or to be constructive …' (Van Zyl Slabbert would have applauded!)

- What did he mean? Beware of extremes – destructive fervour and obstructive obstinacy. All will come right if all reasonable people do their duty, and therein lies a greater reward than to be honoured by people.

- It also speaks of knowledge and acceptance of the fact that he himself would not get recognition. Let the waters go home to Mombasa!

- Then follows his commitment to a democratic ideal, the realisation of which should involve all South Africans: 'When the government in its pursuit of the democratic objective accepted that, apart from own institutions, there should be central institutions in which all individuals and communities should be represented, it thereby accepted by implication that there should eventually be a joint central executive and legislative authority. In accepting the democratic objective and system the government has also accepted that it should be established in a democratic way. When the government chose this option, it thus also opted for a process of negotiation and for negotiated solutions …'

- Then follows his view that the existing systems were inadequate when he says: 'We have become part of systems which we do not like.'
- Inevitably he was, and frequently is, invariably critically, associated with the tricameral parliamentary system, as if that deformed animal represented his political vision. He articulated his own political vision as follows: 'As I see it, this bill should be judged in the light of our common democratic ideal. I ask honourable members to support this bill so that we can have growth and progress on our way to the democratic ideal: a constitution which will be accepted by all because it has been negotiated by all.'

Notwithstanding the fact that PW Botha knew exactly why my father resigned, the author of his biography, *Stem uit die Wilderness*, devoted half a page of speculative obfuscation to the subject. When asked to comment on my father's last speech in parliament, FW de Klerk described it as 'exploratory'.

CHAPTER 14

PW BOTHA'S RESIGNATION

On 18 January 1989 PW Botha had a stroke. Being the most senior cabinet minister, my father was sworn in as Acting State President.

Whilst he was recovering, Botha canvassed an idea with members of his cabinet which essentially boiled down to the question whether he, as state president, should not relinquish his leadership of the National Party. The cabinet members were expected to respond individually. (According to *Stem uit die Wilderness*, Botha had previously, and on a number of occasions, suggested that the workload of the state president should be lightened.)

My father wrote a letter to Botha in his own hand in which he pointed out that he had said, from the outset, that the state president should be above party politics and not also a political leader. He suggested that Botha should request the members of his cabinet to submit a draft proposal as to how the situation could be handled should he resign as leader of the National Party, and which amendments should be made to the constitution. For example, it would probably have been necessary to make provision for a prime minister.

Botha did not wait for an opportunity at which a collective and informed decision could be taken. Instead, on 2 February 1989, a meeting of the National Party parliamentary caucus was informed by letter of his resignation as leader of the National Party with immediate effect. In his letter of resignation, he requested the caucus to fill the position of leader of the National Party to enable him to continue with his responsibilities as state president.

Four candidates were nominated. They were, in order of seniority, my father, Pik Botha, FW de Klerk and Barend du Plessis.

Knowing Botha, my guess would be that he would have preferred a prime minister who would do his bidding, and, since Barend du Plessis was the most junior of the ministers and would in Botha's mind have been less likely to assert himself than the others, he is likely to have been Botha's candidate for the leadership. Botha would probably have discovered in time that he had underestimated Du Plessis.

In the event, FW De Klerk won with only 69 votes against 61 after first Pik Botha and then my father were eliminated. My father immediately volunteered to make way for De Klerk as acting state president so that he could officiate at the opening of parliament the next morning. He was, however, persuaded to stay on in the position.

In my view Botha's decision was unbelievably cynical and stupid. It is clear that he only had his own interests in mind. He must have realised that his illness would add fuel to the fire of those who were already suggesting that it was time for him to leave the public arena. By that time he had already indicated that following the 1989 national elections, he would again be available for the position of state president.

His resignation as leader of the National Party reflects his assessment that his illness was bound to lead to further calls for his resignation and was an attempt to undercut the growing public sentiment that he was overstaying his welcome. It was, however, only a question of time before the intolerable situation which Botha had created would explode in his face.

Early in March Botha gave every indication that he would return to resume his duties, and also that he would serve a further term. This clearly is a matter in respect of which the National Party, of which he was no longer the leader, would have had to take a decision. Daan Prinsloo points out, in *Stem uit die Wilderness*, that in an interview on 3 March with the Cape Town newspaper *Die Burger*, Botha asserted that in his letter of resignation to the National Party caucus he had requested the caucus to consider the separation of the positions of National Party leader and state president, and continued by saying that since the caucus, in its wisdom, elected to endorse his position in this regard, it had assumed co-responsibility. The caucus did no such thing. It was confronted with a *fait accompli*, Botha's resignation, and had no choice other than to elect a successor as National Party leader.

Botha's game was becoming painfully obvious, and later the same day De Klerk said that it was becoming apparent to him that the time for an in-depth discussion between him and Botha was fast approaching.

According to Prinsloo, there was growing insistence, also in the Afrikaans newspapers, that Botha should resign. Botha's answer was to inform my father (in his capacity as Acting State President) that he was going to resume his office on 15 March 1989, three weeks earlier than planned.

In the event, my father was delegated by the senior ministers to present Botha with a proposal which would defuse the situation and leave Botha with an 'honourable' escape. He travelled to George in a South African Defence Force DC3. When he arrived at Botha's residence, he was told that Botha was recording a television interview with Johan Pretorius of the SABC. He had to wait.

The second most powerful man in the country took a car and visited places where he grew up as a boy, to return at 11h00. When they emerged the SABC crew was very excited about the interview that had been conducted in his absence.

Pretorius had to take the video recording to Cape Town because the contents thereof couldn't be transmitted from George. My father was asked whether he would mind (sic) if Pretorius and Ters Ehlers, Botha's private secretary, travelled with him on the plane back to Cape Town.

My father finally saw Botha privately and put the proposal to him. It was that he should call a general election, as a result of which his term would come to an end two years earlier, and be succeeded by FW de Klerk as state president. Botha agreed to this.

On the flight back to Cape Town, my father asked Pretorius what was on the video cassette. Pretorius told him that Botha had said that he would not call a general election. To this my father responded by saying that the video should be destroyed because it would precipitate a crisis in the country, as Botha had told him that he would, in fact, hold an election.

FW de Klerk and other senior members of the cabinet were supposed to meet at my father's residence to be briefed about the meeting with Botha. My mother had prepared dinner for them. No one showed up. I was subsequently told, by Pretorius himself, that he had told FW de Klerk in advance of the contents of the video recording. In the event, De Klerk and his colleagues met elsewhere. I can only assume that they thought my father was somehow co-responsible for Botha's idiosyncrasy. To this day I consider their conduct to have been an inexcusable affront to my parents, in particular my mother. My father resigned a few weeks later.

In the end Botha was forced to agree to hold a general election during 1989, an eventuality which would see him retiring as state president since the National Party had resolved to re-combine that position with that of the leader of the National Party.

Matters deteriorated further, and on 13 August 1989 a number of ministers confronted Botha at his residence where they told him that if he did not resign, the entire cabinet would. That would have left him without a government.

At a cabinet meeting the next morning, a pitiful affair judged by the verbatim record of the proceedings which appears in *Stem uit die Wilderness*, Botha finally indicated that he would resign. That evening South Africans were treated to the spectacle of Botha setting out the reasons for his resignation, and repudiations by De Klerk and Pik Botha.

In *Stem uit die Wilderness*, Prinsloo accounts how my father had to endure severe and unjustified criticism for the role which he had played in the conflict between Botha and the National Party. He also mentions that my father was further implicated in the leadership struggle as a result of a fortuitous invitation which he extended to Johan Pretorius following a working session with Botha at Wilderness. At the Wilderness meeting my father and Botha were supposed to have exchanged views on the matter of the separation of the positions of state president and leader of the National Party.

Notwithstanding the fact that my father had had to endure all the unjustified criticism and never defended himself by telling the truth, Botha never told the truth, not even in his authorised biography.

The truth is this: My father travelled to Wilderness to convey to Botha the cabinet's insistence that he should call a general election and step down. When he got there, Botha was giving an interview to Johan Pretorius. Subsequently he conveyed the message to Botha, who agreed to hold a general election. On the way back to Cape Town, Pretorius told my father that Botha had told him, during the interview, that he was not going to hold a general election. Pretorius conveyed this to De Klerk, as a result of which he and other ministers did not attend a meeting at my father's residence that evening where he was supposed to convey Botha's reaction to them.

Et tu Brute!

CHAPTER 15

RETURNING TO THE FOLD

In the early nineties Piet Riedemann, an attorney attached to the state attorney's offices in Cape Town, told me that Dr Gerrit Viljoen, then Minister of Constitutional Development (Roelf Meyer was the deputy minister at the time), wanted to consult with us. We met in Viljoen's office in Cape Town.

By then Nelson Mandela had been released from prison, the ANC and other unlawful organisations had been unbanned, and the government was squaring up for multi-party negotiations at which a fully democratic constitutional and political system had to be devised for South Africa. To this end the Department of Constitutional Development had already appointed Professor Francois Venter, a constitutional law expert from the University of Potchefstroom, to assist it during the forthcoming negotiations.

Viljoen did not beat about the bush. He asked me whether I could see my way clear to be an expert adviser to the government during the constitutional talks. I said that if the government trusted me with its interests, I would be prepared to take on the task. The matter was settled in principle there and then. It was clear that Viljoen was alert to the fact that I was not a government supporter. I could hardly have been, given the reasons for my resignation as Chief State Law Adviser in the President's Office, related elsewhere, only five years earlier.

There was, however, one snag. I was in private practice as a member of the Cape bar at the time, and could only take on work on the instructions of an attorney. Clearly the intention was that Piet Riedemann had to be that attorney. He, however, insisted that he could not brief counsel to perform a task in which he himself would have no involvement. So it was that I missed out on the first round of talks at CODESA I and CODESA II.

Following the collapse of CODESA II and the Boipatong killings, the continuation of the negotiation process was under extreme threat. However, Roelf Meyer, who had by then succeeded Gerrit Viljoen as Minister of Constitutional Development, and the ANC's chief negotiator, Cyril Ramaphosa, managed to revive the negotiation process – for which the country owes them a great debt of gratitude. Fresh talks, to be conducted in what was styled the Multi-Party Negotiating Forum and its subsidiary organs, commenced in 1993 at the World Trade Centre in Kempton Park.

I was again approached to assist the department and the government as a specialist constitutional law adviser, and this time I resolved not to let the opportunity slip away as had happened previously. In the event, I made representations to the Cape Bar Council to be permitted to act as an adviser to the government during the forthcoming talks without being on brief by an attorney. This permission was granted, and I embarked upon what was one of the highlights of my career.

Almost as if by second nature I was able to find a niche for myself in the department alongside dedicated officials such as Fanie van der Merwe, previously director-general of the Department of Constitutional Development and by then its special adviser, Niel Barnard, previously director-general of the National Intelligence Service and by then director-general of the department, Francois Venter, and a number of young, extremely intelligent and dedicated officials, whose enthusiasm was not dampened by the fact that the majority of them were working themselves out of a job.

I have never worked so hard in my life! First, the government had to get its ducks in a row. It had to go to the negotiating table with some sort of plan and some sort of strategy, and to this end numerous meetings and *bosberade* (bush councils) were held.

I had to become used to – and operate within – an entirely new and unknown environment. Niel Barnard, as senior public servant, headed the AK19 (or however many departmental heads there were at the time), regular meetings involving all the heads of departments. Roelf Meyer chaired the Beleidsgroep vir Hervorming (BGH) – the Policy Group for Transformation. The BGH, which was supposed to be the engine room of the government's constitutional proposal factory, comprised a number of key ministers as well as public servants and specialist advisers. The State Security Council, a very powerful body under PW Botha, which had been rendered a toothless tiger by FW de Klerk, was also still functioning.

In the nature of things, the Department of Constitutional Development would prepare proposals for consideration, first by the BGH and subsequently by the full cabinet. Niel Barnard saw to it that the top public servants were apprised of developments at all times by virtue of his chairmanship of the AK19. He would also convene larger meetings of senior public servants from time to time to achieve this end.

As frequently as necessary *bosberade* would be held involving, depending on the progress that had been made, the members of the BGH only, or the full cabinet and the required public servants and specialist advisers.

It was a deeply divided environment, in the ranks of both the public servants and the politicians. Roelf Meyer wanted the talks to succeed at all costs, and had the bit between his teeth. He counted on the support of the likes of Pik Botha, Dawie de Villiers, Sam de Beer and Leon Wessels. Kobie Coetsee was the most senior minister in the conservative group, although by no means its leader; leaders are made of stronger stuff. Ministers such as Hernus Kriel, André Fourie, Rina Venter and Tertius Delport were all in the conservative camp. If they had had a leader, it would have been Hernus Kriel.

It is, however, somewhat misleading to refer to these groupings as having been enlightened and conservative respectively. In some respects the distinction was more subtle, inasmuch as people like Tertius Delport were more interested in proper checks and balances in the new constitutional dispensation, whereas Roelf Meyer wanted results.

In *The Other Side of History*, Van Zyl Slabbert correctly points out that even in 1992, when De Klerk was forced to hold an all-whites referendum for a mandate to proceed with the negotiations, the National Party used banners which announced: 'Negotiations Yes; Majority Government – Never!' The government and the National Party were set on achieving a consensus-seeking constitutional dispensation with built-in minority vetoes.

According to Slabbert, Roelf Meyer accepted the principle of majority government at a critical meeting of the negotiating committee. When he reported this to De Klerk, the latter was shocked, and apparently said: 'My God, Roelf, you gave the country away.' I remember that particular occasion, although I was not present at the meeting. Meyer told Niel Barnard and me subsequently what had been agreed, and I too was shocked – not because the country had been given away, but because Meyer had no mandate to accept the principle of majority government, given the government's position in this regard.

I was a member of the BGH, and also attended meetings of the AK 19, State Security Council and cabinet as and when the need arose. I considered that my responsibility was to give the best advice I could, and got on with my task without showing any undue regard for bureaucratic hierarchy, as a result of which I made some powerful enemies, but also good friends.

Shortly after my first BGH meeting, at which I incurred the wrath of police commissioner Johan van der Merwe, I had to attend a Security Council meeting. Before the meeting commenced, Dawie de Villiers told me that I could not be as outspoken at that meeting as I had been at the BGH meeting. I was.

I knew Fanie van der Merwe very well from his days as deputy director-general of Justice. He was a good public servant, and to this day is a good friend. I knew Niel Barnard probably as well. He is a good strategist, and probably did a lot more to keep the entire negotiating process on track, particularly by talking to the right, than will ever be known.

Roelf Meyer and I had both lived in Acacia Park, the parliamentary village outside Cape Town, during the first half of 1980 when he was a young parliamentarian and I the Chief

State Law Adviser in the President's Office.

I did not know Francois Venter well, but soon discovered that he was a dedicated academic, well versed in his subjects and, by the time the Multi-Party Forum commenced, thoroughly disillusioned with the artificiality of the constitutional tinkering which had, up until then, been the upshot of the government's attempts to secure a constitutionally guaranteed niche for itself in the new political and constitutional dispensation, as well as with the infighting within the ranks of the government itself. Following the commencement of the multi-party talks, he became the *de facto* chair of the committee that drafted the text of the constitution, and quickly withdrew from meetings involving government representatives, relishing his new task in the company of the likes of Arthur Chaskalson and Bernard Ngoepe.

I hardly knew FW de Klerk at all. He belonged to a younger generation of parliamentarians than my father, who considered him to be one of the best up-and-coming parliamentarians of his time. In 1971 my father invited him to address a youth conference of the Cape National Party at Goudini Spa. I attended this conference, and remember that the theme of De Klerk's speech was the three pillars of separate development. It was fundamentalist stuff, and I did not like it at all.

I drove the car back to Cape Town after the conference, with my father and De Klerk as my passengers. They had an animated conversation, and my impression of De Klerk was that he was an intelligent and courteous man. Over the years he got a reputation as being a relatively conservative National Party member, certainly not one of its enlightened members, a '*verligte*'. (The terms '*verkramp*' – ultra-conservative – and '*ver-*

lig' – forward-looking and enlightened – were coined by De Klerk's older brother, Wimpie de Klerk, erstwhile editor of *Die Transvaler* and later of *Rapport*.)

During the eighties, when my father was Minister of Constitutional Development and Planning, he and his department made earnest efforts to transform South Africa's politics so as to accommodate the political aspirations of all its people fairly and equitably. My father, by virtue of his ministerial portfolio, was chairperson of the Special Cabinet Committee which had primary responsibility for driving this process. (When I later represented De Klerk professionally, he told me that it was remarkable how much had been done during that time to dismantle old-style apartheid.)

I do not think that it will be unfair to say that in that cabinet committee De Klerk would have been the best exponent of a conservative approach, and my father and Dr Gerrit Viljoen, the then minister of National Education, of a more liberal approach.

In *The Last Trek – A New Beginning*, De Klerk himself has this to say on the matter:

> I developed respect and appreciation for the manner in which Minister Chris Heunis managed the sometimes intense activities of the Committee. He was one of the giants of the reform movement, and should receive full credit for the great contribution that he made during the PW Botha period. … I regarded him as a formidable politician with a keen intellect. He too grew to accept me and the contribution that I made. We became a strange team, often at loggerheads, but in the end always able to reach consensus. He tended to attach less importance to

the concept of Own Affairs than some other members of the Committee and I did. As the chief spokesman for Own Affairs, I was often involved in arguments with him. I did not hesitate to confront Heunis on his tendency, on occasion, to adopt too much of a piecemeal approach to constitutional reform. While I could appreciate his need to deliver tangible and visible results, I insisted on looking at the full picture. As with the case of the Coloureds and the Indians, I was looking for a fully principled motivation of reform proposals and a thorough analysis of all the logical consequences of such proposals. Accordingly, I often felt that I had to play the role of devil's advocate – not to slow down reform, but from my perspective to ensure that what we did was part of a clear vision and that we were aware of where it would lead us.

This, unfortunately, reinforced my image as a conservative.

De Klerk would be hard pressed to identify between, for example, Coloureds and whites, a distinction such as would justify the concept of 'own affairs'. It was a cynical device used to engineer a constitutional system which would guarantee that the majority party in the white National Assembly would be the effective majority in the tricameral parliament.

The aforegoing remarks by De Klerk are followed by the following embarrassingly self-serving paragraph:

My position was succinctly described by the American journalist, Patti Waldmeier, in her book *The Anatomy of a Miracle*. She wrote that it was my 'relentless pursuit of logic' which caused me to oppose PW Botha's piecemeal reforms and which sealed my reputation as a reactionary. She quoted Stoffel van der Merwe, a 'verligte' member of PW Botha's cabinet, as saying that I inexorably pressured my colleagues into thinking through the full implications of the piecemeal reforms that they were considering. When I spelled out the implications in this manner, 'everybody shrunk from their proposals'. And then, according to Dr van der Merwe, I was seen as 'the spoiler'.

When my father made his last speech in parliament in 1989 and stated that black political aspirations would also have to be accommodated at national level, De Klerk referred to his speech as being of an exploratory nature, a remark which, certainly by some newspapers, was interpreted as a repudiation of what my father had said.

Whether or not De Klerk had had a Damascus experience, and whether or not he had a mandate for his decision to unban the ANC and other organisations and to release political prisoners, including Nelson Mandela, which he announced on 2 February 1990, the fact remains that he deserves full credit for having taken white South Africa to the point where a negotiated settlement involving all citizens had become inevitable.

According to many newspaper reports, De Klerk denied having been inspired by a Damascus experience to make the announcement which he did in February 1990. However, according to Van Zyl Slabbert in *The Other Side of History*, De Klerk told him, during a personal interview in Tuynhuys, that two reasons motivated him. Firstly, he had made a spiritual leap as a result of which he realised and accepted the moral indefensibility of apartheid, and secondly he would have been stupid not to grab the opportunity which the fall of the Berlin

Wall and the collapse of communism presented. The first self-evidently has all the makings of a Damascus experience.

My own sense of it is that he had realised that, economically, the country could no longer afford to adhere to remaining tenets of the apartheid policy, and that it was about to be brought to its knees by the combined efforts of the international community. This was the major reason that moved him to announce the steps he did. Also, he had discovered that the National Intelligence Service had been in talks with the ANC, both internally and externally.

In the run-up to and during the Kempton Park talks in 1993, I got to know De Klerk relatively well because I had to attend cabinet meetings for the purpose of reporting back on the state of negotiations and receiving instructions.

De Klerk chaired the cabinet well, but was not that good a disciplinarian. For example, although he articulated the cabinet resolutions well, a person like Kobie Coetsee would frequently not adhere to them. This he did with such impunity that I got the impression that he had some sort of hold over De Klerk, because the latter never took him to task for not complying with cabinet resolutions. For example, on one occasion it was decided that a planning session lasting a few days would be held at a military base on the west coast and that all should attend for the full duration. Coetsee, then also Minister of Defence, was not there from the inception. He arrived by helicopter, and stayed only a few hours before leaving again. Only once was De Klerk sufficiently angry to call Coetsee out of a cabinet meeting to reprimand him privately. After a short while the two returned, seemingly as if nothing had happened, and the cabinet meeting resumed. What De Klerk failed to achieve during the run-up to Kempton Park and the duration of the talks was to 'ensure that what the government did was part of a clear vision' and that it was aware of where it would lead to.

The matter of immunity for crimes committed during the apartheid era was high on the political agenda during 1993. Surprisingly the ANC made a proposal in this regard that would have suited government representatives to the hilt. Coetsee, in his capacity as Minister of Justice, declined to accept the proposal, saying that he was working on his own proposal. In the event, as explained by De Klerk in *The Last Trek – A New Beginning*, this matter remained unresolved and could only be articulated by way of a postscript to the 1993 interim constitution stating the parties' intentions in this regard in vague terms. However, De Klerk says nothing about the fact that the ANC had made a proposal that was better than the government could have hoped for, and that Coetsee turned this down.

De Klerk was adept at avoiding confrontation, and I never once saw him lose his temper. On one occasion I actually admired his patience. This was when some members of the Kwa-Zulu cabinet, under the leadership of Chief Minister Buthelezi, met with the South African cabinet in Tuynhuys. Buthelezi started off by reading an hour-long statement severely critical of the South African government generally, and of De Klerk in particular. This was followed by an equally long statement read by Frank Mdlalose, Buthelezi's right-hand man at the time. De Klerk simply listened and responded courteously. In *The Last Trek – A New Beginning*, he has this to say of that occasion:

Our exchange of letters led to a marathon meeting between the IFP and the government at Tuynhuys on 16 September 1993. Buthelezi and his delegation started the meeting with a two-hour harangue, during which they once again attacked the Record of Understanding [which paved the way for the resumption of multi-party talks after the collapse of CODESA] and articulated their deep suspicions that the National Party and the ANC had concluded a secret bilateral treaty. Slowly, during the next six hours, my colleagues and I patiently managed to address the IFP's concerns and to turn the meeting around.

He goes on to relate that the government was able to reach agreement with the IFP to work together to achieve five common constitutional objectives, but, despite this new-found understanding, Buthelezi soon reverted to his old approach when, at the beginning of October, the IFP, the Conservative Party, the Afrikanervolksfront, a coalition of 21 conservative Afrikaner groups, and the governments of Bophuthatswana, KwaZulu and Ciskei formed a new negotiating alliance, which they called the Freedom Alliance.

I personally witnessed how Roelf Meyer and those who assisted him would manage to reach agreement with senior IFP members such as Ben Ngubane and Frank Mdlalose, only to have it torpedoed when Dr Mario Ambrosini, an Italian-American constitutional law expert and Buthelezi's adviser for many years, would approach Buthelezi directly, even there and then from Roelf Meyer's office. In my book there are not many people who undermined the multi-party negotiating process more effectively than Ambrosini.

On the occasion of my run-in with Hernus Kriel (related elsewhere), De Klerk never rebuked Kriel, but did enough to let it be known that he believed me, not Kriel, and that it was up to us to make our peace. I was happy with that, and Kriel certainly could not have been unhappy with De Klerk's handling of the matter because he was shown to have lied to the Security Council.

Naturally the government knew that there was no possibility of a negotiated constitutional settlement that would hold out any hope of it retaining power. That the power would go to the ANC was a foregone conclusion, and consequently much of the preparation for the multi-party talks concerned intricate power-sharing and consensus-seeking models and the protection of minorities, particularly through vetoes and significant provincial powers.

At times these power-sharing models became so artificial and intricate that I did not even bother to try and understand them. The ANC would never have accepted them.

De Klerk, and certainly Roelf Meyer, must have known that many of the non-negotiables solemnly identified by the cabinet would not survive for long. Meyer sometimes did not even bother to state the government's non-negotiable positions in respect of certain issues once he had gauged the ANC's likely reaction.

It has often been said, most recently by Van Zyl Slabbert in *The Other Side of History*, that the ANC had a superior negotiating team. In his recently published book, *My lewe saam met die Suid-Afrikaanse Weermag*, former minister of Defence, Magnus Malan, also takes the position that Roelf Meyer and his team sold the country down the drain and were inferior to the

ANC's team. De Klerk, on the other hand, considers that

> our negotiating teams continued to whittle away at the issues
> that still separated the parties in the negotiating forum. They
> did so with great skill and tenacity, sometimes stretching the
> meaning of words so broadly, and contorting phrases so intri-
> cately, that it was thoroughly confusing for anyone without le-
> gal training.

I have no doubt that Cyril Ramaphosa and those who assisted him were, intellectually and in terms of negotiating skills,
the superior side. However, it was a non-contest for a different
reason. I cannot remember a single occasion when the government or the National Party delegates seriously pressed for
something to the point of actually arguing about it. Being the
government's law adviser, it was not my responsibility to pro-
mote acceptance of its constitutional blueprints, although Niel
Barnard wanted me to take the fight to the ANC; and on occasion I did, only to cause Cyril Ramaphosa to complain that
I was being obstructionist.

Van Zyl Slabbert is right, though, when he says that following the collapse of CODESA II, and in the wake of the
Boipatong violence, the prospects of continued negotiations
were very slim indeed, but were kept alive by Roelf Meyer
and Cyril Ramaphosa.

He is also right in his view that Thabo Mbeki did not participate in the negotiating process. Certainly during 1993 he
did not. I remember at most two occasions when he attended
bilateral talks involving the ANC and the government. There
can be no question that Cyril Ramaphosa was the ANC's chief

negotiator, and that he performed his task admirably; not only because of what he achieved in terms of what the ANC expected to be the outcome of the negotiations, but also because he managed to do so without offending any party to an extent that would have been harmful to the country itself. For example, if Kader Asmal had been the ANC's chief negotiator, there would have been chaos simply because the man listens to no-one and has an ego as large as Table Mountain. Fortunately for all, he only joined the negotiating process very late in the day.

As I have already indicated, frequently, having sensed that something would be unpalatable to the ANC delegation, the government delegation would not even get to the point of stating the government's or the National Party's position, often in respect of matters that had been termed non-negotiable by the cabinet. I saw non-negotiables become eminently negotiable in a matter of minutes. Elsewhere I recount how after an hour's talks with Cyril Ramaphosa, Pik Botha phoned De Klerk to get the go-ahead for a concession to the effect that the TBVC states would be re-incorporated into South Africa before the election. Previously, the government's non-negotiable position was that the TBVC states should be allowed to decide for themselves whether or not to rejoin South Africa, and that they would not be obliged to do so before the election.

I am convinced that De Klerk knew that nothing would come of the sometimes almost ludicrous formulae to protect minority participation in all spheres of government and many of the other non-negotiable positions in respect of certain key issues. In the end he was prepared to compromise with the ANC on the basis of his own inclusion in government at very senior level and that of his closest allies.

Significantly De Klerk expresses the view, in *The Last Trek – A New Beginning*, that he perhaps erred by taking his old cronies with him into the Government of National Unity instead of younger politicians – no doubt he had his protégé, Marthinus van Schalkwyk, in mind when he wrote this. In my view De Klerk erred by, perhaps subconsciously, attaching too much weight to his own capacity to influence the ANC, and secondly by not discounting the fact that he was human and was not going to be there forever. The truth of this is underscored by his ultimate decision to withdraw from the Government of National Unity, a clear sign that he had overestimated his capacity to influence the ANC on key issues.

De Klerk's strategy within his own cabinet was masterful; he simply let things develop. Towards the end of the multi-party talks Roelf Meyer saw me in a corridor of the World Trade Centre at about three o'clock in the morning, and told me to brief the cabinet as to the state of the negotiations at nine o'clock the very same morning. I remember the disbelieving look on the hotel receptionist's face when I asked for a 07h00 wake-up call upon entering the hotel at 06h00.

After my presentation at that cabinet meeting, no member of the cabinet could have had any illusions as to what the state of play was, and that it was a far cry from what they had set out to achieve. Some of them complained bitterly, notably Hernus Kriel, Rina Venter, Tertius Delport, Danie Schutte and André Fourie, who once attacked me viciously at a BGH meeting. My recollection is that he was unhappy with the way in which I had dealt with representatives of the Freedom Alliance with whom I had to meet from time to time, the likes of arch-conservatives such as Mario Ambrosini, Willem Olivier and Fanie Jacobs.

De Klerk simply let them be. He knew that the die was cast and that there was no turning back. I remember thinking that if he had put the matter to the vote, he would probably have lost. But then again, as I have said, there was no turning back, and even the most shortsighted amongst them probably realised that.

De Klerk secured his position in the new dispensation through Section 84 of the Constitution of the Republic of South Africa Act, No. 200 of 1993, which provided that every party holding at least eighty seats in the National Assembly was entitled to designate an executive deputy president from among the members of the National Assembly, and if no party, or only one party, held eighty or more seats in the National Assembly, the party holding the largest number of seats and the party holding the second largest number of seats was each entitled to designate one executive deputy president. In this way De Klerk ensured that he would become one of two executive deputy presidents.

According to De Klerk, writing in *The Last Trek – A New Beginning*, he and Mandela had to resolve the issue of whether the new Government of National Unity would take its decisions by consensus or by a two-thirds majority. Some of his cabinet colleagues very much wanted him to force the ANC to accept the two-thirds option. He, however, favoured a consensus model since he felt that an impossible situation would be created if the cabinet were to have to vote on every matter that came before it. He argues that if the minority parties consistently thwarted the will of the majority, it might in the end have caused intolerable strain on the whole constitutional edifice. In what follows I set out what was finally agreed upon – a far cry from many of the non-negotiable formulae which the cabinet had previously adopted and relinquished as the talks progressed.

In accordance with Section 82(2) of the 1993 interim constitution, the president had to consult the executive deputy presidents in the development and execution of the policies of the national government; in all matters relating to the management of the cabinet and the performance of cabinet business; in the assignment and allocation of functions by him to an executive deputy president; regarding appointments of ambassadors and other diplomatic representatives; and before appointing commissions of enquiry, making appointments in terms of the constitution and other legislation, negotiating and signing international agreements, proclaiming referenda and plebiscites, and pardoning or reprieving offenders.

Cabinet membership was restricted to the president, the executive deputy presidents and not more than twenty-seven ministers appointed by the president.

A party holding at least twenty seats in the National Assembly and which had decided to participate in the Government of National Unity was entitled to be allocated one or more of the cabinet portfolios in proportion to the number of seats held by it in the National Assembly relative to the number of seats held by the other participating parties.

The cabinet had to function in a manner which gave consideration to the consensus-seeking spirit underlying the concept of a government of national unity as well as the need for effective government. Constitutionally the will of the majority party could not be thwarted.

At provincial level, parties holding at least ten per cent of the seats in the provincial legislature, and which had decided to participate in the Executive Council, were entitled to be allocated one or more of the Executive Council portfolios – which could not exceed ten – in proportion to the number of seats held by those parties in the Provincial Legislature relative to the number of seats held by the other participating parties.

The 1993 interim constitution also provided for a Constitutional Assembly which had to pass a new constitutional text within two years from the date of the first sitting of the National Assembly under the 1993 interim constitution. Such a constitutional text had to comply with the Constitutional Principles contained in Schedule 4 to the 1993 interim constitution, and would not be of any force and effect unless the Constitutional Court had certified that all the provisions of the text complied with the Constitutional Principles.

Constitutional Principle XXXII required that the new constitution had to provide that until 30 April 1999 the National Executive had to be composed and function substantially in the manner provided for in Chapter 6 of the 1993 interim constitution. In effect this meant that the Government of National Unity had a guaranteed life up until 30 April 1999, but not beyond that.

Predictably, the Government of National Unity did not, however, live up to De Klerk's expectations. He complains, somewhat naively, as follows in *The Last Trek – A New Beginning*:

> The interim constitution had created room for the president to
> give his deputies special responsibilities. Mandela never chose
> to involve me in any function outside the immediate role that

the constitution had determined for me. I was never asked to represent the country at international meetings or to carry out any task of national importance. Neither did Mandela ever ask me to act as president during his frequent overseas visits. He always ensured that Thabo Mbeki remained in South Africa on such occasions to play his role.

Significantly, De Klerk, who opted for the consensus model, takes the view that debates within the cabinet 'soon began to reveal the flaws and anomalies in the unnatural constitutional coalition within which we found ourselves'.

Apart from blaming Mandela for the problems which the National Party members of the cabinet experienced during the time of the Government of National Unity, De Klerk also complains that the majority of National Party ministers and deputy ministers often failed to tackle the ANC as he would have wanted them to do in the cabinet. Also, they did not fare so well when it came to making a fighting stand against the ANC in opposing decisions which were irreconcilable with National Party policy, as a consequence of which he often felt compelled to join the debate himself to confront the ANC on issues on which there was disagreement. De Klerk believes that this role was a major cause for the growing tension between himself, on the one hand, and Mandela and certain key ANC ministers on the other. In conclusion De Klerk expresses the opinion that he was sorry that he did not give younger and hungrier members of parliament a chance, at an earlier stage, to strengthen the National Party's opposition role in the cabinet.

So it happened that during May 1996, within a week of the

adoption of the new Constitution, the National Party, led by FW de Klerk, decided to leave the Government of National Unity. Although De Klerk expresses the view that the decision to withdraw from the Government of National Unity also resulted in the renewal and rejuvenation of the National Party, it was the beginning of its ultimate demise.

The National Party fared no better outside the Government of National Unity than it did in the Government of National Unity. Following the Constitutional Court's decision not to certify the new Constitution because the 'basket' of provincial powers was not substantially equal to those provided for in the interim Constitution, the National Party's negotiating position *vis-á-vis* the ANC was never better. It now had a very real opportunity to get the ANC to agree to more significant provincial powers, better protection of language rights, better protection of property rights, and better protection of the right to mother-tongue education. Even to the amazement of the ANC, which was sufficiently eager to see the new Constitution certified by the Constitutional Court to make significant compromises, the National Party failed dismally to exploit this golden opportunity.

According to FW de Klerk's autobiography, the Special Cabinet Committee, chaired by my father and especially established to look into the question of the political aspirations of black South Africans, developed a more concise formulation of National Party policy framework 'which constituted a 180-degree change in policy for ever away from apartheid, separate development and racial discrimination'.

According to him, the proposed framework, which was accepted by a special federal congress of the National Party in

Durban in August 1986, 'accepted the fundamental principles of one united South Africa; one person, one vote; the eradication of all forms of racial discrimination; and the effective protection of minorities against domination'. This, according to him, 'sought to strike a balance between the ideal of having one nationhood on the one hand, and the reality of our cultural diversity on the other'. He maintains that the government would have liked to see something closer to the power-sharing in the Swiss or Belgian models.

The truth of the matter is, however, that the government never made a sufficiently forceful stand at Kempton Park and subsequently in its attempts to realise any of these objectives. De Klerk is partly to blame for this because, as I have said, he placed too much reliance on his own capacity to persuade the ANC at the expense of substantive constitutional checks and balances.

CHAPTER 16

KOBIE COETSEE –
MINISTER OF EVERYTHING

Shortly before the commencement of the 1993 multi-party talks at Kempton Park, a full cabinet meeting was held at the Presidency in Pretoria. This cabinet meeting was also attended by officials and advisers, who were assigned to assist the government during the talks. That accounted for my presence there.

The Multi-Party Negotiating Forum was going to be advised by technical committees in respect of the various aspects of the required constitutional reform. The idea was that, even before the general election and the commencement of the new constitution, a Transitional Executive Council, to which certain powers of the cabinet would be transferred, would be established. I was also going to serve on the technical committee destined to advise the Negotiating Forum in respect of the establishment of such a multi-party Transitional Executive Council.

The thought of transferring executive powers of government to a multi-party council was a frightening prospect for many members of the National Party cabinet, a fact that rendered my task very difficult and which caused the progress of the technical committee to be viewed with much suspicion and apprehension

During the aforesaid cabinet meeting, ministers were instructed by State President de Klerk to assign senior officials in their various departments to liaise with me, so that I could be provided with instructions on short notice as the talks progressed. For example, Deputy Commissioner André Pruis was designated by the Minister of Law and Order, Hernus Kriel, to liaise with me for this purpose. Deputy Director-General George Grewar was appointed to liaise on behalf of the National Intelligence Service; and so on.

In the end I got on extremely well with all the officials appointed to convey my requests to their respective ministers and relay instructions to me. There was, however, one problem which caused me (and others) endless frustration. It was this: Kobie Coetsee was the Minister of Defence and of Justice, and was responsible for the National Intelligence Service. These were key departments, and in the nature of things I was going to need instructions from Kobie Coetsee virtually on a day-to-day basis.

I knew Coetsee well. He was a conservative member of PW Botha's cabinet, as he was of FW de Klerk's cabinet. He was an unremarkable, insecure man incapable of one-on-one debate. To this day I cannot understand why Nelson Mandela seemingly holds him in such high regard.

Decisions at the Kempton Park talks were taken on a sufficient consensus basis. In practice that meant that the government and the ANC could effectively veto any progress, because without either's consent there was no sufficient consensus.

It stands to reason that, particularly from the government's perspective, the powers and functions of the Transitional Executive Council involved very sensitive issues since the government was going to have to assign (and in the process lose) some of its powers to a body which it did not control.

At the first meeting of the technical committee which had to draft the empowering (and disempowering) legislation, Fink Haysom, an attorney and law professor at the Wits Law School, and I told the other members that we were not there as uninstructed experts (Dawid van Wyk, Professor of Law at UNISA, for one, was such an uninstructed expert, as was Zenobia du Toit, a Cape Town attorney), but that we represented the ANC and the government respectively. In practice this meant that the committee could only go forward to the extent that the government and the ANC agreed on the various issues at stake. This is not to say that the other members did not make valuable contributions; on the contrary. The point, however, was that without consensus between Fink Haysom and me, no progress was possible. In order for me to be able to agree to proposals, and make my own, I had to have instructions from the responsible cabinet ministers. This meant that I had to get, on an ongoing basis, instructions from, in particular, Kobie Coetsee and Hernus Kriel, since they were in charge of very sensitive and crucial portfolios.

From day one I had countless problems getting instructions from Kobie Coetsee, much to my frustration and also to the frustration of those dedicated officials who had been appointed to liaise with me in order to provide me with such instructions. They frequently expressed their frustration to me and told me that Coetsee, more frequently than not, flatly declined to give instructions.

In order to enable the committee to function, I devised a strategy whereby the committee would draft consecutive reports containing recommendations which I thought would be acceptable to the government, but always subject to the *caveat* that certain aspects still had to be approved by the government – not good from a purely strategic point of view.

From time to time we had to report to the plenary session of the Negotiating Forum on the progress that we had made, and for that purpose we continually updated our reports.

Although Kobie Coetsee and I saw each other frequently at cabinet meetings, and meetings of the BGH (Beleidsgroep vir Hervorming – the Policy Group for Transformation), a cabinet committee, he never spoke to me about the progress that my committee had been making, nor about the fact that he consistently refused to provide me with instructions; this notwithstanding the fact that the BGH was specially established to articulate the strategic planning for the purpose of the government's participation in the negotiating process.

For some reason that escapes me to this day, Kobie Coetsee, quite apparently, did not trust me, notwithstanding the fact that I had been Chief State Law Adviser in PW Botha's office and that we had frequently had to work together. For example, at the very first *bosberaad* that we both attended, he hardly greeted me despite the fact that it had been some years since we had last seen each other.

I was soon to discover that Coetsee was plotting my 'downfall'. He had instructed the state law advisers, who serve in the Department of Justice, to provide him with an assessment and critique of the committee's third report. Contrary to what could rightfully have been expected of him, he did not present this opinion to the BGH, but kept it to himself. His intention was to use it to 'expose' me.

By virtue of my having been a law adviser myself, I still had some friends in the ranks of the state law advisers. One of them realised what Coetsee was up to and provided me with a copy of the opinion which, I should say, did not amount to much. It was clearly an attempt to appease the minister and to provide him with ammunition to shoot down that report.

Following a particular BGH meeting, I was told by the chairperson, Roelf Meyer, that I was required to attend a subsequent cabinet meeting which, as was the rule, was held immediately after the adjournment of BGH meetings. When I was told that the request that I attend the meeting emanated from Coetsee, I realised that he was going to use the state law advisers' opinion on the third report to attempt to discredit me in the cabinet.

I was sitting in the waiting room of the cabinet when Coetsee came out with a broad smile, on his way to the men's room, and said to me: '*Ou Jan, ons sien heeltemal te min van mekaar.*' ('Old Jan, we see much too little of each other.'). To this I retorted: '*Nee, Minister, ons sien heeltemal genoeg van mekaar.*' ('No, Minister, we see quite enough of each other.') He seemed quite taken aback by my response, but did not say anything.

The cabinet adjourned without summoning me. Subsequent to the adjournment I told Roelf Meyer what I had said to Coetsee, and offered to relinquish my brief. Meyer was more amused than anything else by the episode, and insisted that there was no need for me to relinquish my brief or, for that matter, for him to terminate it.

That was not, however, the end of the matter. Instead, a full cabinet meeting, also attended by selected officials, including the deputy chief state law adviser in Coetsee's Department of Justice, Advocate Gerrit Grové SC, was convened for that evening in Pretoria. I was required to attend, which meant that I had to attend to my duties at Kempton Park that day and travel back to Pretoria that evening. (I should say that Grové and I are good friends to this day, and that I hold him in high regard.)

The purpose of the meeting soon became clear. Coetsee was armed with his legal opinion on the third report, and it was apparent that he was going to take issue with me on the contents of the report on the basis of that legal opinion – with the contents of which I was, by then, more than familiar.

What Coetsee, given his limited interest in the progress that was being made at Kempton Park, did not know, was that by then the committee had already produced five more reports in which many, if not all, of the issues referred to in his legal opinion had already been addressed and, to the extent that it had been necessary, remedied.

Coetsee made a complete and utter fool of himself. Each criticism he took from the legal opinion was met with a response from me that that particular issue had already been addressed in one or more of five subsequent reports.

To his credit, FW de Klerk quickly saw the wood for the trees, but allowed Coetsee to soldier on, making a bigger fool of himself while doing so.

At some point, I decided to ask Coetsee about the document he was using. He was obviously obliged to disclose that he had had a legal opinion prepared and that he was using it to attempt to discredit me. I then asked him the obvious question, which was why he had not submitted the legal opinion, if he ever considered there to have been a need for it, to the

BGH. He obviously had no answer to that, but it was quite apparent that those present considered that he deserved the embarrassment he had brought upon himself.

As I have said, what amazes me is that neither on that occasion, nor on others where he similarly had more than enough reason to discipline Coetsee, did De Klerk intervene. There was just one occasion when he got so angry that he called Coetsee out of a cabinet meeting to have a private discussion with him, after which both of them returned and the cabinet meeting resumed without anyone having been told what had transpired between them. It was always my impression, and that of others, that Coetsee had some sort of hold on De Klerk. Of course, De Klerk's strategy could have been simply to allow Coetsee to make a fool of himself, as he invariably did.

The specially convened cabinet meeting at least had a humorous ending. Any lawyer, and many non-lawyers, will know that the test of the reasonable man is an objective test. At some point towards the end of the meeting, and clearly trying to save face, Coetsee pedantically announced that, as everyone knew, the test of the reasonable man is a subjective test! I was sitting next to Gerrit Grové, and said loudly, in a moment of utter frustration: '*Fok dit, Gerrit, ek neem nou nie meer deel aan hierdie "party" nie!*' ('Fuck this, Gerrit, I am not going to participate in this "party" any more!') I should say, for the record, that subsequent to that I never had to deal with a full-frontal Coetsee assault again. However, getting instructions from him remained virtually impossible, and his approach to the multiparty talks unco-operative and destructive.

Nelson Mandela's misplaced admiration for Coetsee can only be explained by the fact that Coetsee had visited him when he was in hospital for a brief spell while still in prison, and subsequently had talks with him. However, Coetsee was one of a number of cabinet members who had to be dragged, kicking and screaming, into the new South Africa.

There is, I think, a lesson to be learned here. Coetsee, in my book, was a weakling, but was nevertheless put in charge of the South African Defence Force, the National Intelligence Service and the Department of Justice and Correctional Service. Notionally he had the means to derail the process which saw South Africa moving from a racially oriented oligarchic state to a liberal democracy.

I often wondered why Niel Barnard, at the time director-general of the Department of Constitutional Development, virtually never participated in the extended channel meetings between Roelf Meyer and his delegation and Cyril Ramaphosa and his delegation, nor in any of the other structured conversations that took place at the time. My guess is that, having identified the dangers to the process, he set about engaging key people behind the scenes in an attempt to lock them in. One such person would have been Constand Viljoen, a former chief of the South African Defence Force and the leader of the Conservative Party at the time. (In *The Other Side of History* Van Zyl Slabbert subscribes to this view.)

But I think Barnard was also alert to what Coetsee was capable of, if he had the balls. Out of the blue and shortly before my departure for Cape Town one Friday afternoon, he asked me whether I would go to military headquarters there to explain to the general staff of the South African Defence Force the state of play at Kempton Park. I agreed to do this, but I confess that it was with some trepidation, and I remember asking the assembled generals and admirals whether they had the power to convert themselves into a court martial — a rather feeble attempt to break the ice.

It was, however, a good strategic move since it gave the people who commanded South Africa's military might an opportunity to receive first-hand information about the progress that was being made at Kempton Park, and what the likely outcome of that process would be.

In the end many questions were asked and answered, and my sense was that at least some of the issues raised by these powerful men were clarified, although their fears might not have been allayed.

CHAPTER 17

HERNUS KRIEL

I did not know Hernus Kriel, Cape leader of the National Party and Minister of Law and Order in De Klerk's cabinet, prior to meeting him during the run-up to the Kempton Park multi-party talks. It had been a long time since I had had any connections with the Cape National Party, of which my father was once the leader.

Kriel, too, was a reluctant participant in the negotiating process, and on one occasion nearly scuppered it when the police carried out an attack on what turned out to be innocent civilians during the talks. Watching him attempt to explain his actions to the Negotiating Forum one evening (he had been summoned by the Forum for this purpose), I suddenly realised that the government had embarked upon a course from which there was no turning back. The idea of a National Party minister having to defend his actions and respond to questions at the non-governmental Negotiating Forum would have been unthinkable even a few months earlier.

In the event Kriel, who had a few stiff whiskies before appearing before the Negotiating Forum, declined to respond to individual questions, but insisted that all the questions be asked and that he would respond to them in one go – a cowardly choice.

My contact person with Kriel was Deputy Commissioner of

Police André Pruis. To the credit of both men I should say that I did not experience the same difficulty getting instructions or directions from Kriel as was the case with Kobie Coetsee, although some of his instructions were quite unattainable.

Kriel was a man who believed in doing things in proverbial style, although I would never commend him for 'style'. At the time I was working virtually around the clock and mostly at Kempton Park, where I stayed at the Airport Holiday Inn so as to be close to the World Trade Centre. Kriel would invariably call for consultations between us to take place before breakfast at his official residence in Pretoria, with him still dressed in his pajamas and dressing gown. No matter how late I had worked the previous evening, I would be required to travel to Pretoria for these early morning meetings.

Pruis, who is still Deputy Commissioner, was a shrewd man who, whilst discharging his responsibilities to the government to the best of his ability, would have been careful not to offend the ANC; but he invariably assisted me to get the mandates from Kriel which I required in order to make progress in the technical committee which drafted the law providing for the Transitional Executive Council.

There was, however, no love lost between Meyer and Kriel, and they had frequent bust-ups, particularly at BGH meetings. At one such meeting Kriel wrote a letter to me in which he said that he wanted to see me after the meeting. I was concerned that there would not be time for us to have a meaningful conversation before the commencement of the next scheduled meeting. For this reason, I sent him a copy of the technical committee's most recent report, which he had not yet seen, and which might have addressed whatever he wanted to discuss with me, and wrote on it the following: 'Minister, this is our most recent report. If there is anything else that you would like to discuss with me, I am at your disposal.' Kriel put the report in his briefcase without looking at it or reading my note.

Shortly before the adjournment of the meeting, Meyer and Kriel had a fall-out which was so intense that Kriel stormed out of the meeting. I therefore had no occasion to speak with him. After the conclusion of the BGH meeting I left for Kempton Park to attend to my responsibilities there. At about lunch time, Niel Barnard arrived to see me. He told me that at the Security Council meeting which had taken place after the BGH meeting, Kriel had told De Klerk, in the plenary session, that I had refused to talk to him despite his request that I do so.

The Security Council meeting was not yet finished, and was due to continue after the lunch break. Barnard insisted that I should accompany him to Pretoria immediately and attend the remainder of the meeting.

Much to my surprise De Klerk asked me to brief the Security Council as to the state of play at Kempton Park, as if this was an item on the agenda, for which purpose I used the recently completed eighth report of the technical committee. I was not interrupted while I did this, and no questions were asked.

After I finished the briefing, De Klerk thanked me and was on the verge of proceeding to the next item on the agenda when I asked whether I could be permitted to say something. I told them that when I was first approached by Dr Gerrit Viljoen, Meyer's predecessor as Minister of Constitutional Development, to assist at CODESA, he asked me whether I could see my way clear to represent the government. I responded by saying that if the government was prepared to trust me with its interests, I would be prepared to do so. As a result of that conversation, an in-principle agreement was reached that I would represent the government at CODESA. I added that that was the way in which counsel worked, and that I had hoped that my relationship with my client, i.e. the government, would be characterised by mutual trust.

However, I had been told that during that morning's session of the Security Council meeting something had happened which, to the extent that such trust existed, had the potential to undermine it. I was informed that Kriel had told the full meeting of the Security Council that I had declined an invitation to meet with him to discuss certain issues.

On my way to Pretoria I had telephoned Noël Basson, De Klerk's private secretary at the time, and asked him to get in touch with Marius Durandt, Kriel's private secretary. I asked Basson to request Durandt to look in Kriel's briefcase where he would find the eighth report of the technical committee which I had given to Kriel that morning, and which he had put in his briefcase without looking at it, or my note on it.

He was also to tell Durandt that there appeared a handwritten note of mine on the first page of that report. I wanted the text of what I had written on my arrival at the Union Buildings. Both gentlemen, who were good friends of mine, obliged, and when I arrived at the Union Buildings, where the Security Council meeting was being held, I was provided with the exact text of what I had written.

I then told the Security Council that what Kriel had said was a lie, and related the story of how I had given him the eighth report with the note on the first page; also, that a major bust-up had occurred between him and Meyer, as a result of which he had stormed out of the BGH meeting without even looking at what I had written.

I then quoted what I had written, which made it plain that I had not declined Kriel's request for a conversation between the two of us. Naturally Kriel had no answer to this, and his embarrassment was compounded by the fact that De Klerk said that it did not sound to him as if I had declined to meet with him. De Klerk added that he was sure that we would be able to resolve the matter amicably between us.

At the Security Council meeting I sat between Niel Barnard and Marius Kleynhans, the Department of Constitutional Development's media liaison officer at the time, who had previously worked for the SABC. He then suggested that I should do what my father would have done and go to Kriel, shake his hand, and tell him that I harboured no ill feelings. I considered this good advice, and did exactly that upon the conclusion of the Security Council meeting.

Kriel was livid. His face was flushed, and I feared that he would have a heart attack. I said to him: 'Minister, in the spirit of what the President said, here is my hand.' He ignored my hand and said to me that I should never ever suggest, in the presence of the state president, that he is a liar. I responded by saying to him: 'Minister, at least I had the decency to say what I had to say in your presence, whereas you told lies about me behind my back.'

Roelf Meyer made an attempt to intervene, on my behalf I assumed, only to be told by Kriel to stay out of it.

To his credit I should say that Kriel did not remain angry

with me, or at least so it seemed. When we next met he acted as if nothing had happened, and I could not sense any hostility or ill feeling towards me.

CHAPTER 18

THE SIEGE OF
THE WORLD TRADE CENTRE

Following the collapse of the CODESA talks, a new initiative based on the Record of Understanding between the government and the ANC was launched in 1993 in an attempt to formulate the basis for a liberal constitutional democracy in South Africa. This culminated in the Multi-Party Negotiating Forum, an assembly of the representatives of the government of the Republic of South Africa, various homeland governments, and various political parties including, of course, the NP and the ANC.

The ultra-right wing in South Africa, as represented *inter alia* by the paramilitary AWB (the Afrikaner resistance movement) of Eugène Terre'Blanche, elected not to participate in these talks. In those quarters the talks were viewed as shameful capitulation to the black majority.

During 1993 the Multi-Party Negotiating Forum regularly met in plenary sessions at the World Trade Centre close to what was then Jan Smuts airport in Johannesburg. Various subsidiary bodies of the Negotiating Forum also convened at the Centre on an ongoing basis.

This was also the place where the so-called 'extended channel' frequently met. The channel comprised Roelf Meyer and Cyril Ramaphosa. The extended channel comprised representatives of the South African government, the National Party, the ANC and the South African Communist Party. The government and the National Party were, as a rule, represented by ministers Roelf Meyer, Dawie de Villiers and Leon Wessels. Fanie van der Merwe, Marius Kleynhans and I represented the government in an advisory capacity.

The ANC and the SACP were represented by Cyril Ramaphosa, Joe Slovo, Dullah Omar, Mac Maharaj, Valli Moosa and Arthur Chaskalson. In terms of intellect and negotiating skills they were definitely the superior team – an assessment shared by Van Zyl Slabbert in *The Other Side of History*, as well as by many other commentators.

Fanie van der Merwe had previously been the director-general of Justice and, subsequently, of the Department of Constitutional Development and Planning, of which Meyer was the minister. He was succeeded by Niel Barnard, the former head of the National Intelligence Service. Van der Merwe's services were, however, retained and he served in an advisory capacity to the Department. Together with Mac Maharaj he was also responsible for the smooth running of the Multi-Party Negotiating Forum. The two of them were very good troubleshooters.

Marius Kleynhans was previously an SABC political commentator, and at this time was the Department of Constitutional Development and Planning's press liaison officer. I was on brief to the government to assist it with legal advice during the duration of the negotiation process.

It is noteworthy that Niel Barnard, at the time Director-General of Constitutional Development and Planning, did not, as a rule, attend these meetings. As pointed out elsewhere, he did behind-the-scenes negotiations with people like Constand Viljoen in order to contain the threat of a right-wing backlash. That this was not an idle threat is evidenced by the fact that the AWB attempted to invade the capital of Bophuthatswana, one of the former independent homelands. This was foiled within a few hours, since the AWB was no match for Bophuthatswana's own defence force.

When I had to attend meetings at the World Trade Centre, I invariably stayed at the Jan Smuts Holiday Inn, only a few kilometres away. Most representatives were taken from the hotel to the Centre by minibus, but since I had to go to Pretoria frequently to attend cabinet meetings, BGH meetings and various other meetings, I had my own car. That being the case, I frequently gave people lifts to the Centre. In the final stages of the negotiations it so happened that I gave Martha Olckers, a National Party representative at the Forum, and Zenobia du Toit, a Cape Town-based attorney, who served with me on the committee that drafted the Transitional Council Act, a lift to the Centre one morning. On our way there I noticed that the route was lined with policemen and that a large number of AWB supporters were in the process of assembling. Many of them were armed with rifles, shotguns, pistols and revolvers; and many of them were already drunk, though it was relatively early in the morning.

The Forum was in plenary session, which meant that all the delegates assembled at the Centre that day. As we approached the gate to the Centre, our progress was hampered by a crowd of AWB supporters to such an extent that the car could hardly go forward.

Martha Olckers, a firebrand if ever there was one, turned

down her window and shouted abuse at the AWB supporters. She had, stupidly, not read the mood they were in. By this time I could no longer move forward or backwards, and I genuinely began to fear that we would be hauled from the car and injured or killed, when a police captain arrived and managed to escort us through the gate of the Centre. Ours was the last car to enter the premises. The huge gates were closed behind us, and the multitude of AWB supporters assembled in front of them. Since the available policemen were stupidly deployed to line the route to the Centre, they were now behind the AWB supporters and there were no policemen between the Centre itself and the AWB supporters.

The gates had hardly closed behind us when the mob forced them open and advanced on the Centre.

The hall where the Forum assembled was on the first floor, in a passage to the left as one came up the stairs from the foyer. Immediately next to this hall were the National Party's offices, and immediately next to them, with an interleading door between, were the government's offices. Roelf Meyer's office was in the middle, surrounded by a corridor that led to some of the other offices.

Having broken down the gate, the AWB mob was unstoppable. They converged on the Centre, and an armoured vehicle drove through the glass entrance doors into the ground floor lobby. I watched from the landing at the top of the stairs on the first floor, with Pravin Gordhan, who is now the Commissioner of the South African Revenue Service. Pravin started shouting at the advancing mob, and I had to drag him away to the government's offices. There were many people in the government's offices. The members of the cabinet present, and their bodyguards, assembled in Roelf Meyer's inner chamber. Cyril Ramaphosa, Joe Slovo, Mac Maharaj, Dullah Omar and Valli Moosa were in a separate office. They had no bodyguards.

The lesser lights, various delegates and personnel, including me, were in the corridor that encircled Roelf Meyer's inner chamber. We were joined there by National Party delegates and personnel.

We had virtually no protection. To this day I believe that violence and bloodshed which could have led to civil war were avoided by two policemen, one a young, but huge, Afrikaans-speaking constable who had played rugby at provincial level, and the other a Portuguese-speaking member of the police who had seen service in the notorious 32 Battalion in South West Africa / Namibia. They were both armed with Uzzis.

They were the only policemen between us and the advancing mob, who were coming up the stairway to the first floor, brandishing weapons.

The two policemen took up position in the corridor in front of the entrance to the government's offices. I was standing in the entrance. The Afrikaans-speaking constable stood upright with his weapon against his shoulder, while the Portuguese policeman knelt and held his Uzzi at the ready.

The moment of truth was when those at the head of the mob spilled into the first floor corridor and turned in the direction of the government offices. It was a frightening sight and situation. The Portuguese policeman shouted at the top of his voice: 'I am going to have to shoot you, I am going to have to shoot you!' At that point, those in front of the mob, who were going to die in a hail of Uzzi bullets, turned into the hall where the Forum met, and were followed by the others, where they assembled *en masse*.

Since there were live broadcasts of proceedings in the Forum on SABC television channels, the cameras were rolling and the entire country could see on television what was happening.

Amichand Rajbansi, the leader of a political party which had participated in the tricameral constitutional dispensation, stupidly went into the Forum hall to fetch his gold pen and was unceremoniously assaulted when he did so.

Since there was an interleading door between the National Party offices and the government offices, entry could be gained to the government offices via the National Party offices. We began to stack furniture against the door to the National Party offices. All of us had become, to all intents and purposes, hostages of the AWB.

After a while Roelf Meyer's private secretary managed to set up a meeting in a National Party office between the invaders and representatives of the government. The meeting was attended by Roelf Meyer, Dawie de Villiers, Meyer's secretary and me. The invaders were represented by Eugène Terre'Blanche (the AWB leader), Constand Viljoen (a former chief of the SADF), Thomas Langley (a Conservative Party member of parliament) and an ultra-conservative trade union leader by the name of De Jager.

Terre'Blanche was boisterous and demanding. He proudly proclaimed that he had taken command of the Centre, although he seemed uncertain as to what his next step should be. After some debate, he put an ultimatum to Roelf Meyer to the effect that his supporters be allowed to leave the building voluntarily, in exchange for which Meyer had to undertake that they would not be arrested. Viljoen did nothing to defuse the situation, and was obviously playing second fiddle to Terre'Blanche.

We asked for time out to consider this ultimatum. When we returned to Meyer's office, Leon Wessels was on the phone to FW de Klerk, and a police general, General le Roux, was present. Meyer asked Le Roux whether he could secure the Centre.

Le Roux responded by telling Meyer how many policemen he had at his disposal, where they would have to come from, and so on. I told him that he wasn't helping the minister. Meyer's question had not been how many policemen he had at his disposal, but whether or not he could secure the Centre. He had no answer to this question, and we therefore had to assume that he couldn't.

I then advised Meyer that he should accede to Terre'Blanche's demand as it would be meaningless, firstly because it would have been given under duress, and secondly because he was not the minister of Police. I told him that the situation was quite obviously explosive and that many civilian lives were under threat. Meyer accepted this advice, and my recollection is that FW de Klerk also approved of this course of action.

There was, however, one problem. Meyer could not give the undertaking without consulting Cyril Ramaphosa and the other ANC and SACP members of the extended channel. In the event, he and I went to see Cyril Ramaphosa and the others in one of the government's offices. Predictably they were dead against the proposal. They were not going to accede to demands from Eugène Terre'Blanche of all people.

I then told Cyril Ramaphosa that what was happening at

the Centre was being broadcast live by the SABC, that his supporters would know what was going on, and that very soon they would be arriving, *en masse*, at the Centre, an eventuality that would most certainly result in a bloodbath. I also told him that Meyer wasn't asking for their approval, but was simply informing them of his intended course of action. On that note we left and returned to the meeting with Terre'Blanche, who, having apparently assumed that his request would be acceded to, had by then ordered the evacuation of the building.

I know that Constand Viljoen, who could be seen on subsequently published photographs running behind the mob in a vain attempt to stop them from entering the Centre, later said that he was almost certain that the Centre was going to be set alight. It would have gone up in flames like a box of matches, since the inner walls were of highly inflammable partitioning.

I remain convinced that an incident which would have had the potential of resulting in bloody civil war was averted through the courage and decisive action of the two policemen.

Shortly after the incident, the Centre swarmed with senior policemen and I was introduced to the investigating officer, General Krappies Engelbrecht. I was asked to make an affidavit concerning what I had witnessed, and I focused on the meetings with Terre'Blanche and his cohorts. After all, he had proclaimed that he had 'taken command' of the Centre.

A few months later I was served with a subpoena to testify in a criminal case against 14 of the AWB members who had participated in the siege. Much to my surprise, Eugène Terre'Blanche was not named as an accused. I phoned the prosecutor and pointed out that the purpose of my affidavit was to assist them with a case against Terre'Blanche; and that there were many other people, who would not have had to come from Cape Town, to testify as to what happened that day.

Given what follows, it is not unsurprising that the state lost its case.

In *Dances with Devils – A Journalist's search for Truth*, Jacques Pauw writes as follows about the aftermath of *Vrye Weekblad*'s first story about Captain Dirk Coetzee, first commander of the notorious Vlakplaas South African Police death squad:

Within hours of *Vrye Weekblad* going on sale that Friday, Max [du Preez] and I were summoned telephonically by a police general. He said he'd been ordered to investigate the death squad allegations. Max and I were curious, and on Sunday morning we made our way to police headquarters in Pretoria.

Wiry and thin-lipped, General Krappies [his nickname means scratchy] Engelbrecht greeted us like long-lost brothers and vowed to get to the bottom of the scurrilous allegations. He wanted the tapes of our interviews and said he would like to speak to Coetzee himself. Would we tell him where he was? Max and I feigned total ignorance about Coetzee's whereabouts and refused to hand over any of our raw material. The whiff of a major cover-up hung heavy in the air of the slimy policeman's office.

As we left, Max said loudly enough for Engelbrecht to hear: 'Fokken valsgat!' [fucking two-faced bastard!] In due course, the general was exposed as not only masterminding the official cover-up, but of having personally ordered assassinations by the Vlakplaas mob and sharing liberally in the spoils of the police slush fund that De Kock and his men had looted for years. Of course Krappies wanted to know where Coetzee was – forty-eight hours after our newspaper hit the streets, De Kock and his most trusted lieutenants had already decided to hunt down and kill the cop who had turned on his own.

Regarding the publication by *Vrye Weekblad* of the confession of another Vlakplaas operative, Ronald Bezuidenhout, concerning his own involvement in an attempt to assassinate Dirk Coetzee by means of a parcel bomb, Jacques Pauw writes as follows:

The day after publication, General Krappies Engelbrecht was on our doorstep. Not surprisingly, he had been appointed to investigate Bezuidenhout's allegations and vowed to get to the truth.

This time, Max told him to his face: 'General, I'm sorry, but we don't believe you.' Unperturbed, he put his arm around Max and said: 'Old Maxie, we are in actual fact on the same side. We both serve the truth.'

Of course, nothing came of his investigations. It took another five years before the full story of the bomb emerged during De Kock's trial in the Pretoria Supreme Court. Every word we had written was true.

CHAPTER 19

ROELF MEYER

I first met Roelf Meyer in the early 1980s. He was a young member of parliament representing a Transvaal constituency, and I was a law adviser to the Department of Foreign Affairs. Both of us had to go to Cape Town for six months of the year during sessions of parliament, and stayed, with our families, in Acacia Park, the parliamentary village to the north of Cape Town.

He was one of the enlightened National Party members of parliament, and we got on well. My middle daughter and his eldest daughter were in the same class at school, and on one occasion shared the honour of being first in their class. We also frequently officiated together at school athletics meetings.

Meyer became Deputy Minister of Constitutional Development and Planning while my father was still the minister. Following my father's resignation in May 1989 Gerrit Viljoen succeeded him as minister, and when Viljoen retired he was in turn succeeded by Meyer. That is how Meyer became the government's chief negotiator in the 1993 Multi-Party Negotiating Forum talks at Kempton Park.

Following the collapse of CODESA and the Boipatong disaster, there was a stand-off between the government and the ANC which could have had dire consequences for the country had it not been for the fact that Cyril Ramaphosa and

Meyer were able to negotiate a document which served as the basis for fresh negotiations, styled the Record of Understanding. Meyer and Ramaphosa became known as the 'channel', and when they negotiated with the assistance of colleagues and advisers they were known as the 'extended channel'. The two of them frequently appeared on television, and worked tirelessly to achieve a negotiated constitutional settlement and to involve as many parties as possible in that settlement.

At the time of the commencement of the Kempton Park talks, I was in private practice as an advocate in Cape Town and, with the permission of the Cape Bar Council, was appointed to serve as an adviser to the government for the duration of the talks. This effectively meant that I became Meyer's adviser as well as that of his department.

During this time Meyer's responsibilities can only be described as awesome. He was responsible for overseeing the day-to-day activities of a very important state department. He was also responsible for formulating the government's constitutional proposals in a political situation in which it was a given that the National Party would be a minority party after general elections involving all South Africa's citizens. He had to get the approval for his proposals in a special cabinet committee styled the 'Beleidsgroep vir Hervorming' (the Policy Group for Transformation). There he had to deal with sometimes very vociferous and angry resistance from the likes of Kobie Coetsee, Hernus Kriel, André Fourie and Tertius Delport. He was also responsible for putting the policy group's proposals to the cabinet under the chairmanship of President FW de Klerk.

His task was immensely complicated by the fact that the

government's official policy ruled out majority rule, as a consequence of which intricate constitutional models had to be devised providing variously for minority participation in government, consensus, significant provincial powers and more. His task was further complicated by the fact that the cabinet would frequently determine that certain of its proposals were to be regarded as non-negotiable in circumstances in which Meyer (and certainly also De Klerk) must have known that the ANC would never agree to those proposals. His task furthermore involved negotiating principally with the ANC, its alliance partners, and also with the other role players at Kempton Park which, with few exceptions, viewed the entire process with a not-inconsiderable degree of scepticism.

At the time Meyer was a boyish-looking, bright and studious man. He had an unflappable temperament, and I have no recollection of him ever losing his temper, notwithstanding the fact that I have seen him in situations in which he was severely provoked.

I would not have wanted to be in his shoes. His schedule was hectic. His safety was a source of real concern, given the fact that there were many threats against his life. Few were grateful for what he was trying to achieve because he was regarded either as a sell-out to the ANC, or not a match for his ANC counterparts. Not even all his colleagues were grateful for his efforts, not to speak of being impressed by them, and he also had to bear the brunt of FW de Klerk's anger when things at the talks were not going the way he wanted them to go.

I served with Meyer on the extended channel and was therefore privy to the negotiations between the government and the ANC. I also attended negotiations between the government and other parties which were conducted by Meyer and, sometimes, assigned to me.

On a personal level he got on well with most people, with the exception only of Patricia de Lille. Within five minutes of the commencement of a meeting between the two of them, one or the other would storm out.

To my surprise, I got on well with De Lille as well as with the other representatives of the PAC at the Negotiating Forum.

On occasion, after the Appellate Division's decision in the *De Lille v The Speaker of the National Assembly* case, in which I represented the Speaker, De Lille and I were having an animated conversation on the sidewalk in front of the Huguenot Chambers in Cape Town. A young lady attorney approached, gave us one look, and said: 'My God, now I have seen everything!'

Meyer had nerves of steel. On one occasion, and to commemorate a special day for the town council of the Strand in the Cape, the cabinet held its regular meeting at the city hall in the Strand. It was one of those endless meetings at which various terribly artificial constitutional models and formulae were discussed. That evening Meyer had to appear with Cyril Ramaphosa on an SABC television programme. I did not think Meyer had any chance of being in time for his Johannesburg interview.

Because of the safety considerations to which I have already referred, Meyer's official vehicle would normally drive very fast, with the vehicle transporting his security guards right on its tail. After the cabinet meeting, Meyer was taken to Cape Town International airport, and I drove with the security guards in the rear vehicle at speeds of up to 180 kilometres per hour.

We were transported from Cape Town to Waterkloof Air Force Base in Pretoria by Lear jet. On arrival I got into my car and drove to the Airport Holiday Inn at Kempton Park, and Meyer was whisked away to SABC headquarters in Auckland Park. When I got to my hotel room I switched on the television in time to see the commencement of the interview with Meyer and Ramaphosa.

Meyer was tireless, and frequently worked through the night. Shortly before the talks at Kempton Park concluded, he saw me at 03h00 and asked me to brief a cabinet session on the state of play at Kempton Park at 09h00 that same morning.

The only occasion on which he admitted to being tired was during the last night of the talks at Kempton Park when everything had to be wrapped up. He came to me and asked me to represent the government in a full plenary meeting. There I was, being advised by ministers and stating the government's position on matters that were still outstanding, including financial matters of which I knew more or less nothing! I remember that, against my advice, the meeting decided to change the name of KwaZulu-Natal to Natal only. It is a matter of public record that that decision had to be overturned to induce Chief Minister Buthelezi to participate in the general elections the following year.

Meyer was also very loyal, and stuck by me when I had serious bust-ups with the likes of Kobie Coetsee, Hernus Kriel and André Fourie. He had good relationships with officials. They were not scared of him, but they respected him and my sense was that they enjoyed working for him.

As recounted elsewhere, it has frequently been said, by

knowledgeable commentators such as Van Zyl Slabbert, that Meyer and his negotiating team (Dawie de Villiers, Leon Wessels, Fanie van der Merwe and I) were no match for Cyril Ramaphosa and his team (Joe Slovo, Dullah Omar, Valli Moosa, Mac Maharaj and Arthur Chaskalson). Objectively I would say that they were the better team, but not necessarily the more cohesive. However, there was never anything approaching an argument during the talks with the ANC delegation, and frequently Meyer, having taken the sense of the ANC's likely reaction to a proposal or a position, would not even put it.

I was not present when Meyer agreed, at Kempton Park, that the constitution should provide for majority rule. When he subsequently reported this to Fanie van der Merwe, Niel Barnard and me, I could not believe what I was hearing; not because I was opposed to the concept of majority rule, but because it was an absolute no-no for the government. Reportedly FW de Klerk was outraged when he heard about it, and told Meyer that he had sold South Africa down the drain.

In the end the guarantees that the government were able to get accepted did not amount to much. They were, by and large, contained in the Constitutional Principles with which the new constitution had to comply, and were invariably vague and uncertain.

Meyer's most significant achievement was the fact that he was able to revive multi-party negotiations, to keep them alive, and to bind in the most significant role players in the country – no mean feat considering all the centrifugal forces at work in South African society at the time.

During the negotiations I realised that the ANC had an understandable distrust of the South African public service, assuming that it had a deep-seated loyalty to the apartheid regime and ideology. This was far from the truth, especially as far as many of the most senior and competent public servants were concerned. In those days South Africa had a good public service, and especially its senior public servants (particularly in departments such as Constitutional Development, Finance, and Foreign Affairs) rated among the best in the world and had no ideological commitments to the government. They simply did their job to the best of their ability and in the interests of the country. Yet many of them were the first to leave the public service after the ANC took over the governance of the country. They invariably held senior positions, to which the ANC wanted to appoint their own candidates, and accordingly they were offered severance packages to vacate these positions. There is every indication that, in time, the ANC government realised that it would have been better to retain their services and, by so doing, their experience, because they were uniquely placed to assist during the transition period. As a consequence many new appointees to the public service did not have the benefit of the intellect, experience and guidance these gifted officials had to offer. As a result of this, the quality of South Africa's public service today ranges from appalling to mediocre at best. This is likely to remain the case for many years to come.

If there was one thing that the government ought to have attempted to protect, apart from its own backside, it was the quality of South Africa's public service. There would have been many logical and morally defensible underlying reasons for such insistence. That, however, did not happen.

Following the Constitutional Court's refusal to certify the

text of the 1996 draft constitution, there was a golden opportunity to get the ANC to agree to more significant constitutional safeguards and provincial powers. In my view, Meyer
did not capitalise on this opportunity, and even went on holiday during the time when negotiations regarding appropriate
amendments to the 1996 draft constitution were being negotiated with the ANC.

Considering who and what he represented, his relatively junior status in the cabinet, the divisions within the government itself, the legitimate expectations of the vast majority of the South
African population, and the powerful interests at play, Meyer is,
in my book, much more of a hero than a villain.

Following my father's death, Meyer is reported to have said:
'He was the right person at the right place at the wrong time.'
I take this to mean two things. Firstly, it is an acknowledgement of the fact that my father was hamstrung by constraints
which Meyer himself did not have to contend with. Secondly, at the 'right time' my father would have been the 'right
person' to conduct negotiations aimed at the transformation
of South Africa to a fully democratic state. Be that as it may,
it was always a foregone conclusion that the multi-party negotiations would yield a constitutional dispensation providing
majority rule. Meyer could not have avoided this outcome,
but could and should have done more to secure constitutional
protection of minority rights, particularly following the Constitutional Court's refusal to certify the first constitutional text.
Meyer's legacy is that he did not allow the negotiations to
falter and realised, sooner than his cabinet colleagues, that it
would have been futile to resist the ANC's insistence that the
constitution should provide for majority rule.

CHAPTER 20

THE 'SUNSET CLAUSE'

One of the ANC's advisers at Kempton Park was Professor Nicholas (Fink) Haysom, an attorney in the partnership of Cheadle Thompsom & Haysom and an associate professor at the law school of the University of the Witwatersrand. In many respects he was my counterpart at the multi-party talks, although he was not a regular ANC member of the extended channel, i.e. the ANC delegation led by Cyril Ramaphosa which negotiated bilaterally with the government delegation led by Roelf Meyer.

As could be expected, much of the work at Kempton Park was done in committees according to guidelines laid down by the plenary session of the Multi-Party Negotiating Forum and which ultimately had to be approved by that body. Over and above our other responsibilities, Fink and I served on the committee which had to draft the legislation providing for an interim executive council which would function pending the coming into force of the interim constitution and the holding of elections in terms thereof.

At the very first meeting of our committee, we both declared that we were not uninstructed experts but on brief to the ANC and the government respectively. The other members of the committee showed remarkable understanding for our position, and they knew that the committee would only be able to move forward once Fink and I, or rather our principals, were able to reach consensus. This is not to say that they did not press their own ideas; on the contrary.

The committee's task was not without problems. To the government the whole idea of sharing power, albeit in the interim and albeit not supreme executive power, with the ANC and other parties and in respect of important matters such as defence and law and order, was virtually unthinkable. The ANC, on the other hand, did not want the Transitional Executive Council, as it was called, to be, in Cyril Ramaphosa's words, a toy telephone. As always, a balance had to be struck.

I suspect that my task was more difficult than Fink's task, if only because I had such difficulty getting instructions from Kobie Coetsee, the minister of Defence and of Justice and Correctional Services. Be that as it may, with the able assistance particularly of our colleagues Dawid van Wyk, professor of law at the University of South Africa, and Zenobia du Toit, a Cape Town attorney, and Anton Meyer SC, a deputy chief state law adviser, we were able to finalise our draft law in good time. I remember the evening when we put the final touches to it; Fink walked through the corridors of the World Trade Centre with a bottle of Roelf Meyer's finest scotch whisky in his hand, taking swigs as he went.

In the beginning I was extremely irritated by Fink's casual demeanour. The committee would normally be scheduled to meet at 09h00 on Monday mornings. I would travel from Cape Town and be in time for the meeting, only to sit with the others and wait for Fink who would maybe rock up as if nothing was the matter at 11h00 or later. Upon his arrival he would invariably pour himself some coffee and have some cookies before sitting down to begin with the (rest of the) day's work.

Fink knew that I had severe difficulties with my principals, particularly Kobie Coetsee, and as matters progressed and the understanding between us developed, I had no doubt that he conveyed to the ANC leadership the constraints under which I had to work.

We were forthright with each other in our dealings, and a relationship of trust soon developed between us. On one occasion when Dullah Omar dogmatically resisted the idea of a minister co-signing documents which had to be signed by the president being written into the constitution, I explained the obvious need for this to Fink and Arthur Chaskalson, and they prevailed upon Omar to relent.

At the time of the negotiations, Fanie van der Merwe was employed by the Department of Constitutional Development and Planning as a specialist adviser. Previously he had been the director-general of the departments of Justice, Home Affairs and Constitutional Development. He knew the public service inside out, and had a good sense for political strategy.

Van der Merwe, Mac Maharaj (who had served his prison sentence with Nelson Mandela on Robben Island and was the source of wonderful anecdotes about him) and, initially, before the Inkatha Freedom Party and the KwaZulu government withdrew from the negotiations, Ben Ngubane, were responsible for the smooth running of the Kempton Park talks. They were very adept at resolving conflict, and the country owes them a great debt for defusing potential threats to the talks and keeping everything on track.

From the inception of the talks, Van der Merwe kept pestering me about a 'sunset clause' – impressing upon me that the talks could be an unqualified success and yet sink on the question of the sunset clause. Technically it was not a proper sunset clause, but that is how we referred to it.

I was working so hard at the time, frequently getting to bed only in the early hours of the morning, that I did not do anything about the sunset clause, although I realised that Van der Merwe was right. Van der Merwe's fear was obvious and realistic. In the event of a deadlock, the probability was that the Defence Force would take over control of the country, an event that would most certainly have led to outright civil war.

One evening, Van der Merwe having cornered me and Mac Maharaj having cornered Fink, they brought the two of us together in an office in the World Trade Centre, impressing upon us, at some length, the need for a sunset clause. After a while I jokingly told Mac Maharaj to bugger off since they were wasting our time, and Fink and I commenced drafting what became Section 250 of the 1993 interim constitution, the sunset clause. By two o'clock the next morning the sunset clause was done.

In essence it provided that if the Independent Electoral Commission declared that it was unable to certify that any elections, i.e. national or provincial, were substantially free and fair, the Commission had to declare either that it was able to determine a result based on the votes which could be counted, or that it was unable to determine any result.

If the Commission was able to determine a result, a new election had to be held for the National Assembly and the provincial legislatures or a particular provincial legislature as soon as practicable, but not later than twelve months after the date of the first election.

In such eventuality, parliament and the provincial legislatures had to be established on the basis of the result which the Commission was able to determine, on condition that no provincial legislature could be established unless the National Assembly was established. Parliament was disqualified from amending the Constitution, the Independent Electoral Commission Act, the Electoral Act, the Independent Media Commission Act or the Independent Broadcasting Authority Act until such elections had been certified as substantially free and fair. Provincial legislatures established on the basis of a declaration by the Commission that it was able to determine a result based on the votes which could be counted, had no legislative competence in the interim, save for the power to enact laws necessary for the appropriation of revenue or monies and the imposition of taxation.

If the Commission was unable to determine any result, fresh elections had to be held for the National Assembly and the provincial legislatures, or a provincial legislature, as soon as practicable but in any event not later than ten weeks after the date of the first election. In such event the constitutional arrangements provided for in the Republic of South Africa Constitution Act of 1983, the Transitional Executive Council Act and the various acts pertinent to elections, as well as the Independent Broadcasting Authority Act, would continue to apply until the election had been held. The continued existence of the Electoral Commission was also provided for. Nothing was left to chance.

Fortunately, our sunset clause was never needed, but it had to be there. If the elections, for whatever reason, did not yield an outcome, or were not substantially free and fair, there would have been a constitutional road to follow.

INDEX